'Testing, Testing ...'

ASSESSMENT IN ADULT LITERACY, LANGUAGE AND NUMERACY

A NIACE POLICY DISCUSSION PAPER

**Peter Lavender
Jay Derrick
Barry Brooks**

niace

promoting adult learning

promoting adult learning

©2004 National Institute of Adult Continuing Education
(England and Wales)

Reprinted 2004, 2006

21 De Montfort Street
Leicester
LE1 7GE

Company registration no. 2603322
Charity registration no. 1002775

NIACE has a broad remit to promote lifelong learning opportunities for
adults. NIACE works to develop increased participation in education and
training, particularly for those who do not have easy access because of class,
gender, age, race, language and culture, learning difficulties or disabilities, or
insufficient financial resources.

You can find NIACE online at **www.niace.org.uk**

Cataloguing in Publication Data
A CIP record of this title is available from the British Library

Designed and typeset by Patrick Armstrong, Book Production Services,
London
Print and bound in the UK by Latimer Trend
ISBN 10: 1-86201-193-1
ISBN 13: 978-1-86201-193-9

Contents

Acknowledgments

Peter Lavender's paper was originally presented at the Economic and Social Research Council Seminar Series 'Linking Research, Practice and Policy in Adult Basic Education', organised from Edinburgh University by Lyn Tett, Mary Hamilton and Yvonne Hillier. Jay Derrick's paper developed from discussions at the seminars. Barry Brooks' paper is unrelated to the seminar series. Further details of the seminar series, the original papers and summaries of the discussions can be found on the website at http://www.education.ed.ac.uk/hce/ABE-seminars/.

Introduction

There is now, across the whole field of public service, increased recognition that targets are a mixed blessing. In their favour, they offer a clear focus for service providers, often beset by a plethora of options. They encourage a focus on the outcomes of services, and they can secure significant change in practices. Above all, the existence of measurable targets is an important lever in discussions with the Treasury about the release of new resources. The difficulty, in education as in health, is that the need for service providers to meet externally determined targets can distort their behaviour – privileging the needs of the provider over those of learners. The problem was summed up, graphically, at the beginning of the literacy campaign of the 1970s by Tom McFarlane. The problem is, he suggested, 'you teach what you test.' For the Skills for Life strategy to succeed, the teaching needs to address the full range of learner need, and, in time at least, assessment tools need to be available and recognised to capture the full range of learner achievement.

On the other hand, there has also been a long tradition of basic education tutors protecting learners from the intrusion of external scrutiny – sometimes at the expense of giving learners opportunities to have their real achievements externally recognised. At its worst, that led to a culture of dependency on individual tutors.

Three external factors have had some influence on the development of the national targets in literacy, numeracy and language. Firstly, the rules applied to adults have been shaped by the concerns about assessing the achievement of pupils in initial education. Since externally set and assessed tests were seen as obligatory to assure the quality and consistency of young people's qualifications, the legal remit of the Qualifications and Curriculum Authority limited its power to recognise qualifications to programmes with formal external assessment. There can be arguments about the applicability of this definition to young people's education, but it is, in our view, unnecessarily limiting, given the complexity of experiences, purposes, and learning contexts in which adults learn. That case was heard for the first time in more than a decade in 2003, with QCA's floating of proposals for a discrete assessment regime for adults. That can only be welcome.

The second factor was political. The success of targets in securing rapid improvements in school results during its first term of office led the government to adopt formal Public Service Agreements, linking the release of money to the achievement of prescribed learning goals. It is something of a triumph that the Skills for Life targets have been achieved so impressively in the first two years of the PSA regime. But this is in no small measure the result of the design of the target, and the inclusion of young adults' results in the numbers counted. NIACE has argued from the first adoption of the PSA target that the government needed to complement its achievement target with a participation target – to recognise formally that to get 750,000 people through the national tests by 2004 would require 2,000,000 people to participate in literacy, numeracy, and language studies; and double that number to be involved to enable the 2007 total to be achieved.

Thirdly, the implementation of the Skills for Life strategy relies on decisions made by local Learning and Skills Councils. The LSC has a remit across the range of workplace, college and community further education. Yet its staff was drawn disproportionately from the Training and Enterprise Councils it succeeded. TECs were responsible for some 15 per cent of the LSC's curriculum range, and had a powerful transaction culture. Identifying and achieving targets was central to their business: the nuances of successful strategies for widening participation perhaps less so.

When the Skills for Life policy was adopted NIACE welcomed it warmly. No one who has been involved with the long struggle to secure adequate well resourced learning opportunities for adults to study literacy, numeracy and language can be in any doubt that the national strategy has marked a huge step forward in Britain. For too long, too much provision was a hole-in-the-corner affair, backed by inadequate teaching, training and resources, as inspection results from 1994 testified. The adoption of national standards, a clear curriculum framework, the provision of training programmes and the development of national tests have all contributed to improvements in the offer to learners, as Barry Brooks argues eloquently here.

NIACE recognised the real achievements and the compromises necessary in achieving the national tests we do have, given the context outlined above, and we have encouraged people to use the opportunities they provide. Nevertheless, it is essential that the tools we have command the maximum level of support among learners, teachers, awarding bodies, and the wider public. To that end there must be a case for extending the assessment regime beyond reading to other dimensions of literacy, and to other modes of assessment, too, building on the base we have now, and that we develop a portfolio of measures that locate numeracy in context. It is essential, too, that the funding mechanisms adopted reflect the participation dimension of that strategy, as well as the achievement of targets, to help guide local practice. Once these tools are in place it may be easier to persuade local LSCs to fund the proper range of studies, and for tutors to encourage learners to take the tests.

As a contribution to the debate necessary to secure development, NIACE is pleased to publish three linked policy discussion papers. In the first, Peter Lavender explores how narrowly drawn LSC guidance on funding and priorities risks distorting a generously drawn national policy. In the second, Jay Derrick looks at the relationship between formative and summative assessment and literacy learning. In the third Barry Brooks analyses the challenges confronted and progress made in identifying national standards and tools of assessment. In publishing them we hope to contribute to a debate about how best Britain can meet the policy goal that underpins the target – how best can we strengthen skill and confidence in literacy, numeracy and language among all those adults in Britain who need support and encouragement.

Taken together the three papers remind us that each policy and procedure is the result of choices, whether consciously made or not, which are political, and privilege some interests over others.

NIACE believes the debate over measurement is of real importance. It is practical politics for all who can benefit from taking the national tests as they currently exist to be encouraged and supported to do so. And the recognition the tests provide offers learners who can benefit from clear milestones on their on their learning journeys. But it is also practical politics to want to improve the tests so that they offer those benefits to all learners.

Alan Tuckett
Director, NIACE

Tests, targets and ptarmigans

The ptarmigan is a kind of grouse living in alpine and arctic tundra areas throughout the northern hemisphere. Ptarmigans have feathered toes to help them walk across the top of the snow. Although all three ptarmigan species have been studied by scientists, their levels of tolerance to human-induced changes remain largely unknown. They are a favourite prey for huntsmen, whose techniques take advantage of the fact that ptarmigan drag their feet in soft snow. A series of snare loops are tied into a long line, and the loops are placed flat on the ground around a favourite thicket of willows. Birds step into the loops, drag their feet forward – and are caught.[1]

Overview

This paper is mainly about government targets and national tests in relation to the national 'adult basic skills strategy' and social inclusion, in England.[2] It is also about how the best of intentions can lead to disaster. Like the ptarmigan's feet, the national targets have been designed for the best of reasons but could lead ultimately to poor outcomes.

The story so far

In *A Fresh Start* (1999)[3] Sir Claus Moser and his committee noted how impressed they were with the new national targets for literacy and numeracy at Key Stage 2 in schools, particularly in the way in which they motivated and generated action. They believed that a similar approach was required for adults. Several reasons were given:

* To complement the existing strategies for schools
* To follow up the national target for increasing participation in basic skills programmes set out in *The Learning Age*[4]

---

1   Aniskowicz, 1994.
2   This paper is entirely about policy in England, even though the word 'national' may be used.
3   Moser, 1999.
4   DfEE, 1998. The figures given were 500,000 per annum learning in basic skills programmes by 2002.

- To encourage long- and medium-term improvement towards reducing by half the level of poor basic skills by 2010, through:
  - raising functional literacy in England from 80 per cent to 90 per cent
  - raising functional numeracy in England from 60 per cent to 70 per cent.[5]

The Moser Committee urged the government to devise:

a national target for key skills as soon as robust measures have been developed (5.10)

The 'robust measures' were not spelled out, but the challenges were clear: such an improvement would only bring England to the level of where Sweden is today. Ambition was balanced with realism. The targets, they decided, ought to make allowances for people who had learning difficulties, immigrants, those for whom English is not their first language, the reduction in the number of young people leaving school with poor basic skills, and those who '*may have no desire to improve*' (5.14). The committee's proposed targets were entirely related to levels of literacy or numeracy skill in the adult population, but the focus was on achieving the participation target of 500,000 in programmes; these targets to be refined following a proposed baseline survey. The committee suggested the target percentages shown in Table 1.

Table 1. Possible targets for 2005 and 2010 (percentages)[6]

	Now	2005	2010
Literacy			
All adults	80	84	90
People aged 19	83	90	95
Numeracy			
All adults	60	64	70
People aged 19	60	85	90

The Committee made several recommendations. The first was about a national strategy but the second recommendation was about targets:

(i) *As part of the National Strategy, the government should commit itself to the virtual elimination of functional illiteracy and innumeracy.*

---

5 The achievement of these targets would '*lift 3.5 million out of low literacy… [and] 3.5 million out of low numeracy*'. It would '*get 9 out of 10 people to a level where they can undertake Level 1 literacy tasks effectively, and … enable 2 out of 3 adults to complete simple numeracy tasks*' (5.11).

6 Moser, 1999, op. cit. section 5.15. There are definitional problems here but the original text is still worth consulting.

> (ii) *In addition to the accepted participation target for 2002, the government should set specific basic skills targets for adults and for young people to be achieved by 2005 and 2010, on the scale proposed in the new National Strategy.*

The participation target was important but the committee recommended that other targets be devised, following a baseline survey. The baseline survey commissioned by the government in 2002 reported in 2003.[7]

The government's response to *A Fresh Start* was to accept the recommendations for a national strategy, and to create a unit inside the DfES. The new strategy, *Skills for Life*, was revised in 2003.

The revised national strategy *Focus on Delivery to 2007*[8] starts with a reminder of *A Fresh Start* and the figures that Moser reported. The purpose has shifted from participation, though, to qualifications, albeit with an echo of the international comparisons:

> *Our goal is to reduce the number of adults in England with literacy, language and numeracy difficulties to the level of our main international competitors – that is from one in five adults to one in ten or better. We aim to help 750,000 adults achieve national certificates by 2004, and to help 1.5 million achieve the same by 2007*[9]

Perhaps the most enlightening section of the *Focus* document on 'Learner Achievement' is the government's comment,

> *It's not enough just to help them reach levels of functional literacy, language and numeracy. Our strategy aims to improve their skills up to and including Level 2 of the National Qualifications Framework, whether they choose to follow programmes leading to qualifications in literacy or numeracy or key skills*[10]

The strategy does *not* recognise that learners may not wish to follow a programme leading to a qualification. The choice is between 'key skills' and 'literacy, language or numeracy' (not working towards a qualification or not). In addition, it is clear that reaching levels of functional literacy, as suggested by the Moser Committee, is now no longer the goal. The new focus is to become qualified, to improve 'skills up to and including Level 2...'. It is not clear where this shift in emphasis has taken place.

The *Fresh Start* report had recognised that both portfolio and test-based methods of assessment have their strengths and weaknesses. The link between formative and summative assessment is a crucial part of the learning process for most learners. The Moser Committee argued that coursework assessment is attractive to learners who would be put off by having to take a test, helps teachers to provide effective feedback and is a motivating process for learners (10.23). On the other hand, the report

7   DfES, 2003a.
8   DfES, 2003b.
9   DfES, 2003b, section 5.
10   DfES, 2003b, section 12.

argued, assessment through coursework may make it harder to ensure uniform standards; tests have the advantage of greater objectivity; they might lead to greater credibility with employers; and might be attractive to adults who may want to learn on their own (10.24).

The committee argued that any new qualifications should be based on the new national adult literacy and numeracy curriculum, another parallel to the Key Stage 2 arrangements in schools, and be subject to rigorous moderation and national standardisation (10.26). Coursework-assessed qualifications would continue, alongside the new national tests, provided they were based on the standards from which the national adult literacy or numeracy curriculum had been devised.

This parallel arrangement (portfolio and test-based methods) has been marginalised in more recent guidance from the Department for Education and Skills, although key skills qualifications do have a course-based component, of course.

A Fresh Start also warned about what might happen if the qualifications were to become a dominant focus:

> *All methods of assessment are open to abuse and some have been abused in the past. The funding methodology of various funding bodies has over-encouraged programme providers to get people through the qualification. Coaching – or insufficiently rigorous standards in assessment of coursework – has been a problem. Similarly some programmes have 'taught the test'; people have sometimes passed specific entry tests for very specific occupations in this inadequate way. (10.25)*

Fresh in their minds was the early inspection evidence on adult basic skills. The evidence reported that there was a proliferation of qualifications, some of them virtually worthless, and that in some cases students were doing qualifications solely because it was believed that without qualifications the course could not be funded. On many occasions since, this misunderstanding has been corrected. Again, the Moser Committee's recommendations were crisp and clear:

> (ii)   *Only basic skills qualifications based on this new curriculum should be funded from the public purse. Whether assessed by coursework, test or a mixture of both they should use a common set of standards laid down by QCA.*
>
> (iii) *Existing qualifications should be revised to meet these new national standards.*
>
> (iv)   *Existing qualifications based exclusively on tests should be replaced by a new National Literacy Test and a new National Numeracy Test both available at Levels 1 and 2.*
>   (Recommendation 16 – Curriculum and Qualifications)

The committee's intention was that basic skills qualifications would be based on the new national curriculum; that all basic skills qualifications should conform to this arrangement and that they could be assessed by coursework, test or a mixture of both. It did not state that an end test should be the exclusive form of assessment.

Out of focus?

The most recent iteration of the national strategy for improving adult literacy and numeracy skills moves far beyond the original Moser Committee proposals. In many ways this could be expected. Four years on, however, the government's intentions do not suggest that continuous assessment is an option. In the 2003 DfES publication *Focus on Delivery to 2007* it is made clear that 'achievement' means 'national qualifications'[11] and these mean end tests. The 'key elements of the learning infrastructure' from pre-entry level to level 2 are set out as:

- screening
- initial assessment
- diagnostic assessment
- learning materials
- tests and qualifications.

Since September 2002, all literacy, numeracy and ESOL learning programmes '*have had to be based on the National Standards for Adult Literacy and Numeracy to attract Learning and Skills Council funding*'[12]. The standards, or 'fixed benchmarks', are described as 'broadly equivalent to the attainment expected of seven-year-olds, 11-year-olds and GCSE grades A*–C respectively'. The echo from the Moser Committee and the new Key Stage 2 target is unmistakeable.

Although *Focus on Delivery to 2007* argues that learners should be encouraged to '*commit to their own learning*'[13] this is not quite the same as taking some responsibility for it. However, the expectations on all providers are good ones:

> *... to draw up an Individual Learning Plan (ILP) with each learner which sets out the learning aims, the learning goals and the smaller 'steps' that the learner will take in order to achieve their goals. Learners can also expect to have a teacher who gives regular, positive, recorded feedback, and who is able to use a full range of teaching approaches, from group work, to one-to-one and online learning.* (112)

It is a short step to make this teaching methodology a part of both the formative and summative assessment process and an integral part of the identification and recording of achievement.

But in order for national qualifications to match the expectations on providers we need more than a national test. The government suggests that we don't:

> *Since September 2001, many learners embarking on a literacy or numeracy programme leading to Level 1 or Level 2 now work towards the National*

---

11   See DfES, 2003b, 'Learner achievement' sections 108–24.
12   DfES, 2003b, section 109.
13   DfES, 2003b, section 112.

Test. For teachers familiar with other qualifications… this signals a major change…. Closely linked to the national standards and curriculum, they provide a clear and reliable measure of a person's achievement. Tests leading to National Certificates in Literacy and Numeracy at Level 1 and 2 are available through many awarding bodies. (120)

The tests at Level 1 and 2 are multiple-choice and machine-marked, providing immediate feedback on-screen. Qualifications at Entry level have also been devised by QCA, and these also involve assessments which are independently or externally set or validated, externally marked or moderated, and are conducted under supervised and specified conditions. They only have to contribute at least 50 per cent to the overall award, however.[14]

National PSA adult basic skills targets

Tests as a proxy for achievement are here to stay, not least because of the way in which the national PSA target for adult basic skills is to be measured. A long way from the Moser Committee's recommendations, the adult basic skills targets are related only to the achievement of national qualifications in basic skills and key skills at level 1 and 2 and adults achieving English and mathematics GCSE. The Secretary of State for Education and Skills, Charles Clarke, refers to the 'formidable targets' of 750,000 adults achieving a qualification by 2004 and 1.5 million by 2007. Closely linked is the 'record spending' across government of £1.6 billion over three years.[15] It is not clear how the figure is arrived at, given the activity in every department. Nevertheless it is a substantial amount[16] and without it we would not have this unprecedented spending on adult learning. As Jane Mace puts it:

And we agree that we are glad. After so long at the margins, at last there is a feeling that the job of providing fulfilling adult basic education is moving centre stage.[17]

The national target brings with it substantial opportunities for potential learners, for providers and for widening participation. The link between funding and the PSA target is key to understanding the conundrum about basic skills qualifications. PSA targets are about measurement and improvement. Just counting numbers of learners would not indicate any progress being made: so the government has to find another quantitative measure. But does the achieving of these qualifications ('National Test')

---

14   QCA website: National Adult Literacy and Numeracy Qualifications – Entry Level.
15   DfES, 2003, Foreword.
16   It contrasts interestingly with the £10 billion that 'poor literacy, language and numeracy skills are estimated to cost the country', DfES, 2003b, Foreword.
17   Mace, 2002.

indicate that learners are making progress? Clarke says that he wants '750,000 adults to improve their literacy, language and numeracy skills by 2004'. The best that can be promised is that many of these learners will indeed make progress as well as pass the test, but there is no assurance that this is so, no causal link between progress made and test passing – especially when anyone can take the test on-line. All will depend on the quality-assurance processes – inspection, strategic area review, self-assessment – together with the expectations on all providers mentioned above. The achievement of the PSA target, then, depends not on everyone learning, not on their commitment to learning, not even on the progress measured in their Individual Learning Plan, but on the achievement of those learners who pass the national test. And it is possible to count only one of these qualifications – passing a level 2 qualification straight after level 1 will not count. It is imperfect but it is what we have got. Not much harm there, except perhaps that it will underestimate by a very long way the real achievement and participation of learners such as those at pre-entry and entry level, and there is the risk, posed by the Moser Committee, of the test corrupting the curriculum in some way.

Tests, qualifications and funding

The strategy and the PSA target has an unhelpful side-effect on the national basic skills qualifications; exactly that predicted by the Moser Committee. The Learning and Skills Council funding method is starting to 'over-encourage programme providers to get people through the qualification'.[18] Similarly, some programmes have 'taught the test', and some local offices of the Learning and Skills Council are threatening to fund only provision in which learners are to take the test. All of the local LSCs have a target to meet, set by the LSC as a proportion of the 2004 national target. Consider this guidance from the Learning and Skills Council and the DfES:

> *Local LSCs are now rightly concerned to move a significantly greater amount of their providers' literacy, language and numeracy provision to that which counts towards their achievement target.*[19]

Any provision for literacy, language or numeracy based on the national standards and not leading to an approved, national qualification is defined by the LSC/DfES as 'other provision'. No expansion of 'other provision' can happen without *'early'* discussion with the LLSC[20] and 'other' provision is discretionary – each LLSC can decide when and how much to allow. Providers are also reminded that the funding of qualifications 'approved for inclusion in the National Qualifications Framework (NQF) as a key priority in order to meet its challenging basic skills and level 2 and

---

18   Moser op. cit. 10.25.
19   DfES/LSC, 2003.
20   DfES/LSC, 2003, page 2.

3 targets'.[21] The full text of the fact sheet issued by the LSC and DfES together allows for a little more flexibility than is immediately apparent from these points. 'Other' provision is intended to be used to encourage those not ready for a qualification or where the 'main purpose of provision is to widen participation'.[22] However, the limitations attached to 'other' basic skills provision is given heavy emphasis:

> *...learners' abilities should not be underestimated, and if it later becomes apparent that the learner could gain a qualification, providers should take action to transfer them to qualification-bearing learning*[23]

The tone is clear. It would be unusual for learners to be taking a basic skills course and not do a qualification, except where the purpose of the course is to 'widen participation'. Any course not offering a qualification might prove hard to defend during an inspection or audit. And the qualifications, as I have said, depend on an end test, even at entry level.

But are the tests inadequate? Jay Derrick argues in his paper that they are no better or worse than any other summative assessment of their kind. They do what tests with no context will always do: provide a rough measure of some reading or maths levels. However, this is a long way from the good practice emphasised by the government in *Focus on Delivery to 2007* where,

> *Learners can ... expect to have a teacher who gives regular, positive, recorded feedback, and who is able to use a full range of teaching approaches, from group work, to one-to-one and online learning.*' (112)

The quality of the tests might improve but without a connection between the formative and summative assessment they may not help learners to 'commit to their own learning'. The tests will need to be revised and improve in their match to the national curriculum. Considering the literacy national test, Jane Mace[24] notes:

> *This is an exercise about measuring... But it is not a test of literacy. To call it such must be regarded as an abuse of language. This is a test not of literacy, but of reading, and of a very particular kind of reading at that. And it embodies a mistaken (and dangerous) idea that truly literate people always write alone, unaided and without mistakes, and that anyone else is lacking "basic skills"... it has nothing to do with the real world where people read and write. In the real world (rather than the artificial one of tests), experience and research both tell us that everyone engages in literacy within a social context, and often that context implies cooperation, not solitary testing.*

---

21   DfES/LSC, 2003, page 2.
22   DfES/LSC, 2003, page 4.
23   DfES/LSC, 2003, pages 2 and 4.
24   Mace, 2002.

Without a good-quality test (and maybe they are as good as they can be, given the early stage of their development), with the pressure of a funding method, and with priorities lying with one form of measuring achievement, what can be done to offer good-quality 'other' provision which puts learners first?

Tests, national targets and social inclusion

'Other' provision simply means literacy, language and numeracy provision that does not lead to an 'approved' qualification. Its purpose is to widen participation or form part of the social inclusion agenda. *The Learning Curve* (2002)[25] tries to identify 'what works' in neighbourhoods in order to reduce social exclusion. It is part of the comprehensive learning and development strategy for neighbourhood renewal. Encouragingly, *The Learning Curve* does not try to say that one size fits all – *different people need different learning tools that encompass more than formal training*. The report identifies closely inter-related problems: lack of adequate childcare facilities and pre-school learning; poor school attendance; low pupil/parent expectations; high rates of school exclusion; low levels of educational achievement; low levels of participation and qualifications; and low levels of literacy and numeracy among adults.[26] Intervention suggestions include 'provision for adult education and lifelong learning' (note the 'embedded' model of provision). To widen adults' participation in learning, it is suggested, requires:

> *effective information, advice and guidance (IAG) [which] can make a major contribution... Gaps in basic skills... need to be addressed with some tact and imagination... Some projects have found it more productive to use a 'gateway' course – e.g. on ITC skills – as a means of providing people with a comfortable environment in which to come forward. Community-based provision is particularly important here.*[27]

How different in tone from the guidance on recording adult literacy, language and numeracy provision! *The Learning Curve* is one of many publications on what works in relation to widening participation. If the models of provision are flexible enough for those hardest to reach, why can't we use such models for everyone else? If we make it right for these learners and potential learners, might we not get it right for all, and might we not have a better chance of meeting those targets?

Every year surveys tell us that a significant minority of adults do not perceive that they have participated in learning since they left school, and a huge majority of these say they have no intention of doing so in the future. The numbers of adults participating in learning remains relatively unchanged year after year. Those most

---

25   Office of the Deputy Prime Minister, 2002.
26   Office of the Deputy Prime Minister, 2002, page 6.
27   Office of the Deputy Prime Minister, 2002, page 8.

advantaged by initial education, wealth, good health, and social class, do more. Those with least purchase on the system do the least learning after school. It has been observed many times that the suggestion of a national test is not a motivator for adults who are not traditional participants in adult learning. In themselves, the tests will not widen participation unless they bring with them some kind of opportunity perceived by the individual to be of value.

What is needed is a way of measuring achievement which motivates and sustains learners in their commitment to their own learning. We need to link together the good practice which learners can expect in the use of formative assessment with summative assessment and a valued qualification. The assessment needs to be in a context recognisable to the learner, as the government suggests,[28] and in tune with the learners' interests and requirements. To reduce the risk of the ptarmigan effect – of twisting the curriculum and the funding of provision out of shape – the government could usefully continue to focus on the numbers of people actually learning as well as those achieving qualifications. Counting the numbers involved in learning would give a guide to the scale of the response from the public. If the government needs a picture of *progress* towards the PSA or Moser Committee's targets then a measurement of levels of literacy and numeracy in the population could be determined by regular omnibus survey. This is done for the adult participation data. Together, these figures could be more useful for Treasury funding purposes and offer less risk that only certain kinds of learning in literacy, language or numeracy is regarded as valid.

Measuring in more than one way allows for a more rounded picture. If we don't do this we can fall into the trap of thinking that a simple figure can tell us answers about progress, participation, success and achievement. It can't. As Charles Handy (1994) noted in *The Empty Raincoat*, the Macnamara Fallacy suggests that,

> *The first step is to measure whatever can be easily measured. This is OK as far as it goes. The second step is to disregard that which can't easily be measured or to give it an arbitrary quantitative value. This is artificial and misleading. The third step is to presume that what can't be measured easily really isn't important. This is blindness. The fourth step is to say that what can't be easily measured really doesn't exist. This is suicide.*[29]

This was five years before the Moser Committee reported. It is clear that better and more accurate counting of one thing will do no more than measure one aspect of what is there; it won't widen participation, increase the numbers of people learning or improve the quality and effectiveness of what they learn. If the funding only values one aspect of provision, even though it might recognise 'other' kinds of motivation for learning literacy, language or numeracy, then the 'abuse' feared by the Moser Committee will become a reality.

---

28   DfES, 2003b, section 112.
29   Handy, 1994, page 219.

Conclusion: the ptarmigan's feet

A Fresh Start (1999) recommended national targets for literacy and numeracy levels for adults. These targets were related to overall literacy and numeracy levels in the population, complemented the strategies for schools, and aimed to raise participation. The '*Skills for Life*' strategy, revised in 2003, contains targets related not to participation but to qualifications achieved by learners at levels 1 and 2. The goal was not necessarily to improve functional literacy, language and numeracy, as the Moser Committee proposed, but to improve skills and the numbers of people with qualifications up to and including level 2. The Moser Committee had recognised that qualifications based on coursework and on tests were appropriate, provided that both were based on the new national adult literacy and numeracy curricula. *A Fresh Start* warns that too close a focus on qualifications can distort the curriculum. Recent government strategy documents refer only to end-test qualifications as the means of valuing achievement. However, there is recognition of the importance of formative as well as summative assessment. This is not carried through to policy implementation, since local Learning and Skills Councils have been told to favour the funding of qualification-bearing courses in adult basic skills above those that are not. The recording of the numbers of people passing tests is only a proxy for the measurement of achievement. This recording will not in itself measure progress, only individual achievement, and even then only achievement of a certain kind, since the national tests are free of context and free of any link with formative assessment. The national tests do, however, offer an easy way to create a target and draw down very welcome resources. Without them we would have made even less progress towards a lifelong learning culture.

This paper concludes with the observation that, in themselves, the national tests will not widen participation because they are an inflexible way of measuring individual progress and of encouraging more and different people to participate. What is needed is a balance of ways of measuring achievement available to learners, and a more flexible use of opportunities that make a link between formative and summative assessment, such that the assessment is in a context recognisable to the learner and in tune with the learners' interests and requirements. The collection of participation data, with regular national surveys on literacy levels, would give a better and more accurate national picture. This is more in tune with what the Moser Committee suggested, easier for administrators to fund, and less open to the kinds of abuse of the curriculum noted by the Committee in 1999. The ptarmigan's feet are perfectly constructed for what they need to do. Sadly, the simplicity of their design is also their downfall, since they make the ptarmigan easier to track and snare. So it is, I think, with the national targets: the shift of focus to a test might distract attention from participation, from real measures of achievement, and from the proper learner-centred curriculum.

Some questions

1   How significant is the link between formative and summative assessment?
2   What could be done to enhance the existing basic skills qualifications, to make them more congruent with how the best teaching should be?
3   Is it possible to have a national test which accurately measures literacy, numeracy and language in context, enhances learning, and at the same time provides accurate data on national literacy and numeracy levels?
4   How can we make the national expectations on providers for good-quality teaching and learning match the national expectation on how achievement should be measured?
5   What are the research questions which need to be asked in order to make sure that policy is properly built on research, in relation to tests and targets?

Acknowledgements

I am grateful to those who offered critical feedback, advice and support in the production of this paper: Jay Derrick, Jan Eldred, Barry Brooks and Alan Tuckett.

Peter Lavender

Making the grade:
assessment and achievement in adult literacy, numeracy and language

Summary

This discussion paper surveys the present arrangements for assessment and the measurement of achievement in adult literacy, numeracy and language in England and Wales. It points to the complexity of the field, and the diversity of approaches to assessment that can be found, due to the field's interconnectedness with a wide range of curriculum areas and contexts, each of which has distinct traditions and priorities. It identifies and discusses a wide range of relevant research activity. The paper then looks in detail at assessment *of* learning, the measurement of outcomes in adult literacy, numeracy and language, and identifies two fundamental problems produced by the organisational complexity of the field and the range of different stakeholders: firstly, that using measured outcomes of learning for funding and performance-measurement purposes creates a vicious circle in which, over time, all learning tends to focus only on the summative assessment process, so that in the end all that is being measured is effectiveness at 'passing' the assessment. The second problem follows: this cyclical process does not have the learner at its heart: rather, it diminishes learning, and tends to demotivate learners. The last section of the paper is constructive: it looks at assessment *for* learning, and the practices of formative assessment which can be used to support and enhance present and future learning, particularly for 'low-achieving' learners. The paper suggests identifying elements of the present systems for assessment that (a) inhibit learning and (b) enhance learning, and concludes with recommendations intended to help remove the inhibitors and support and develop the enhancing factors.

The purpose and structure of the paper

This paper is intended as a contribution to the continuing development of the national literacy, numeracy and language strategy *Skills for Life*.[30] NIACE wholeheartedly supports the objectives of *Skills for Life* as part of its commitment to adult learning and to widening participation in learning in general. We welcome the energy and resources that have been deployed since the inception of the national strategy in January 2001, and applaud what has been achieved over the past two years, in terms both of galvanising activity and of providing a coherent framework for that activity. We endorse the broad sweep of the strategy to define standards and a curriculum for literacy, numeracy and language, to encourage the participation of new learners through partnership working between agencies and providers, to raising standards in teaching and learning, and to achieving the national targets for achievement. NIACE will continue to support the ABSSU by managing training and development projects within the national strategy, and by contributing to policy development, research and evaluation. In the context of this paper, NIACE is committed to contributing to the development of systems for the assessment of learning which are efficient and effective from the point of view of all stakeholders, and particularly for learners.

This paper is organised in four sections. The first section covers the national strategy and the targets; the range of settings in which adult literacy, numeracy and language is taking place; the varying approaches taken historically across post-16 education and training to assessment and the measurement of achievement, and a brief survey of relevant research activity. In the second section the paper discusses assessment *of* learning: how learner achievement is measured, and the role played by these measurements in funding systems and in institutional performance measurement. This section argues that these functions of assessment have significant impacts, for better or worse, on both the organisation of learning and on learner motivation, and that this needs to be more fully understood in policy approaches to assessment and the measurement of achievement, if unintended problematic effects are to be avoided. The third section of the paper looks at assessment *for* learning, and the ways in which assessment frameworks and practices can actually add value to learning, rather than just taking a snapshot of it at a particular moment. The final section of the paper makes recommendations for future research and development.

The national strategy and targets

While this paper makes a range of recommendations for the improvement and strengthening of the present framework for assessment within *Skills for Life*, NIACE believes that learners in the system at present should have the opportunity whenever

---

30   DfES, 2001.

it is appropriate to have their achievements recognised and celebrated. This may be through one of the national tests or by one of the other assessment processes recognised as valid and relevant to learners. It is important that learners themselves should retain the right to choose whether, when and how their achievements are assessed. The political importance of the national *Skills for Life* targets is such that no opportunity should be missed to support the effort to reach them, and NIACE calls on everyone involved in literacy, language and numeracy to do everything in their power to support adults who are at the appropriate levels of attainment to take a relevant qualification, whether it be the national test, a Key Skills assessment, or a GCSE in English or mathematics.

NIACE has also recommended, however, that the national target for achievement in adult literacy, numeracy and language should be complemented and enriched by a national participation target.[31] Although the overall message of the evidence on attainment in adult literacy and numeracy for the UK is alarming, NIACE has argued for years that an even more profound problem for us is that of low participation in post-compulsory learning, as described in *The Learning Divide* publications.[32] This view, echoed in the Kennedy Report,[33] *Learning for the Twenty-First Century*,[34] the Green Paper *The Learning Age*,[35] and *Skills for Neighbourhood Renewal*,[36] is that increasing participation in learning of any kind is a critical and more challenging target, so far unachieved since 1996.[37] We would also like to see the achievements of all learners, not just those working at the higher levels, recognised by being included in the overall target.

Range of contexts for literacy, language and numeracy (LLN) learning

The context in which assessment and the measurement of achievement in literacy, language and numeracy takes place, is complex. The LSC sector, launched in April 2001, brings together learning across the whole range of adult and further education, and training in the workplace. 'Adult learning' encompasses non-accredited learning (previously known as non-Schedule 2 provision), and accredited programmes which since the 1992 Act have been formally part of the FE sector. Much of adult education is informal, takes place in community settings and is at the cutting edge of efforts to widen participation in learning among people who are described as socially excluded. A significant body of work takes place in prisons, and is the subject of a recent far-reaching policy discussion paper published by NIACE.[38]

---

31   NIACE, 2001.
32   Sargant *et al.* 1997; Sargant 2000.
33   Kennedy, 1997.
34   Fryer, 1997.
35   DfEE, 1998.
36   DfEE, 1999.
37   Sargant and Aldridge, 2002.
38   Uden, 2003.

'Further education' involves both 16–19 year olds and adults, includes Advanced Level and General National Vocational Qualifications study, vocational training courses in all occupational sectors, foundation degrees and a wide range of professional training. 'Workplace training' includes all National Vocational Qualifications work. Adult literacy, language and numeracy learning takes place in all these contexts and settings, and can take the form of *discrete* programmes of literacy, numeracy and/or language; of specialist *learning support* in literacy, numeracy or language for learners enrolled on 'mainstream' programmes; or be *embedded* in vocational or community development programmes in which literacy, numeracy or language is integrated within course learning plans, assignments, and assessment. Closely related and overlapping is the area of 'Key Skills', which is the subject of a distinct though connected set of policies and practices. Also closely related is 'Adult and Community Learning', which is presently the subject of intense research and debate over the most effective approaches to assessment and the measurement of outcomes: often it is not intended to lead to external qualifications.

Approaches to assessment and the measurement of achievement

These different sectors have quite different histories in relation to assessment and the measurement of achievement. Historically, liberal adult education has tended not to lead to formal qualifications, though since the 1980s pioneering work by the Open College networks has developed sophisticated techniques for moderating and assessing adult learning against goals set by the learners and teachers themselves. Since the 1992 Act and before, there has been a trend within adult learning to embrace external qualifications, though it is difficult to generalise about these in terms of approaches to assessment, as they vary so widely. City and Guilds qualifications, for example, tend to mix moderated teacher assessment of coursework assignments with externally marked assignments or tests. AEB literacy and numeracy qualifications consisted solely of externally set tests. GCSEs have changed from being assessed wholly through end-of-year unseen examinations, towards a varying proportion of internally marked moderated coursework assignments. The range of approaches to assessment within further education is nearly as broad as the range of qualifications (approximately 25,000) delivered. In the workplace, the competence-based assessment approach of NVQs is the best known, but is by no means the universally accepted model.

A further important contextual factor is the relative market value of the range of qualifications available to learners in adult literacy, numeracy and language. It is clear that at the lowest levels of learning, the main function of external qualifications is to give recognition to learners' achievements, rather than conferring advantage in the employment market, for example. In theory, the higher the level at which achievement is made, the more market value in employment terms qualifications in adult literacy, numeracy and language have. In practice, this is, in fact, doubtful, because the best-known qualifications in English and Mathematics at Level 2 are GCSEs, which act as a symbolic target for achievement for very many adult literacy, numeracy and language learners, precisely because of their wide currency. In the employment market it is likely that other qualifications in English or Mathematics at Level 2 or below merely demonstrate that the learner has *not* achieved a GCSE, and thus could in practice damage their employment opportunities.

The problem is that these qualifications on their own do not qualify anyone to do anything in particular: either they need to have credibility as reliable indicators of an agreed level of general education, or they need to be achieved alongside, or embedded in, other qualifications which confer specific vocational skills, such as catering or construction. Reflecting this problem, many employers are looking in prospective staff for a spectrum of skills, aptitudes and attitudes within which abilities in language or maths are an integrated part: some of the wider elements of this spectrum have been referred to as 'soft key skills'. These employers may see qualifications narrowly-focussed on adult literacy, numeracy or language as insufficient evidence of employability anyway. Many learners at levels 1 and 2 are quite sensibly aiming to achieve GCSE qualifications rather than specific basic skills qualifications such as the national tests, as they have more credibility as general education in the employment market. Others are looking for vocational qualifications within which relevant literacy, language or numeracy skills are embedded.

From the learners' point of view, the wide diversity of approaches to assessment across the post-school sector is largely immaterial. The learner wants to feel that the method of assessment in their learning programme is valid and fair, that the outcome fits with their own assessment of what they have achieved, and that their achievement is suitably valued and recognised. The wide range of qualifications available (albeit much reduced by the national strategy) and the significant differences between them in assessment schemes and market value, contribute to confusion among learners, employers and providers. This has been exacerbated by the illogical policy situation on what counts towards the national targets: literacy, numeracy and language learners' achievements below Entry 3 do not at present count, whereas achievements by 16–18-year-olds at key skills in communications and application of number, and by adults at GCSE, are counted. This is particularly inconsistent because entry-level programmes are fully funded by the LSC, learners' achievements at those levels do draw down achievement funding for providers, and they are included fully in the data used for institutional performance measurement and inspection.

Research insights from neighbouring fields

A number of key recent British research projects, many of them led by NIACE, have reported on various aspects of assessment and identifying, recognising and measuring achievement in adult learning in general as well as in the context of basic skills.[39] As this paper was being written, the national research project on Planning

---

[39]   Dewson *et al.*, 2000; Greenwood *et al.*, 2001; Grief and Windsor, 2002; McGivney, 2002; Turner 2001; Turner and Tuckett, 2003; Turner and Watters, 2001; and Ward and Edwards, 2002.

Learning, Recording Achievement (PLRA) in literacy, language and numeracy, led by LSDA, was nearing completion. Developing Embedded Basic Skills (DEBS), an action-research programme led by NIACE looking at best practice in supporting literacy, language and numeracy learning within workplace, vocational training, and community learning settings, was about to publish its final report. Important recent studies on assessment in adult literacy work have also been published in the USA.[40]

At the same time, parallel debates are taking place within wider contexts of learning. A recent study of the development of autonomy and motivation in GNVQ students and the critical role of formative assessment[41] has direct relevance for adult learners, including and especially those improving their literacy, language or numeracy. The work of the Assessment Reform Group,[42] though primarily focussed on approaches to assessment within schools, links this to lifelong learning through studying the effects of different kinds of assessment practice on the present and future motivation of learners, and especially low achievers within the schools system. Also important is research on workplace learning, much of which attempts to understand and improve the acquisition and assessment of skills transferable from one workplace context to another: literacy, language and numeracy are clearly paradigmatic in this context.[43] For example:

> *We know that the idea of simple skills transfer from one setting to another is very problematic – the fact that we can use common language to describe a skills group does not mean it is transferable intact. What we need to understand better is the processes by which skills are 'transformed' from one setting into another. Naive mappings of key skills from one environment into another are not a basis for occupational mobility. Even 'near' transfer into related activities is far from simple…*[44]

The two main positions in the key conceptual debate within adult literacy, numeracy and language, between 'situated practices' and 'generic/autonomous' views of skills and their use and acquisition, are linked by the idea of 'transferability', which suggests the question 'How can transferability of literacy, numeracy and language skills between contexts be assessed effectively?' For what is the point of learning these skills if they cannot then be used within and between different contexts? Finally in this survey of relevant research, we need to take account of the growing range of studies on informal learning, in which the same issues of assessment and measurement of progress in learning are even more problematic.[45]

It is clear from an overview of this research that there is a growing body of evidence across a range of different studies, that some approaches to assessment and the measurement of achievement in adult literacy, numeracy and language have the potential to play a significant role in improving attainment in adult learning in

---

40   For example Merrifield, 1998; Beder, 1999; and Sticht, 1999.
41   Ecclestone, 2002.
42   ARG, 2002.
43   Eraut, 2002; Evans, 2002.
44   Evans, 2002.
45   Coffield, 2000; Evans, 2002.

general and in literacy, numeracy, and language in particular. However, this potential is unlikely to be realised by prescribing particular assessment methods and excluding others. All approaches to assessment for learning have their uses and are part of the 'arsenal' of techniques and processes available to teachers and learners.

The research suggests rather that the key problems are with two aspects of the overall framework within which assessment takes place at present. The first problem is the powerful evidence for the negative effects on learner motivation of standardised testing used for summative assessment. These effects are produced in two ways: through public comparison of peer learners' achievements, and through the experience of failure, and are more pronounced the more learners lack confidence in themselves as learners, i.e. the less success they have had in learning. The second problem is the use made of assessment outcomes in allocating funding and in measuring the performance of providing organisations. This produces an overemphasis in professional culture on assessment of learning, teaching to the test and so on, at the expense of assessment for learning, assessment which actually improves learning. The tension between the potential for assessment to contribute to learning and to inhibit it is explored in the next two sections of the paper.

Assessment of learning: measuring achievement in adult literacy, language and numeracy

While sympathetic to the idea of a national target, NIACE is concerned that the achievement of this target will drive provision more than the needs of learners. The former is quantitative, and the latter is both qualitative and quantitative.[46]

The issue is not whether we should assess to summarise learning but rather how we should do it.[47]

We now look at the assessment *of* learning: how successful has the learning process been? The answer to this question is important for a number of quite different stakeholders. First and foremost among them are learners, who want to know what they have achieved, who deserve recognition of their learning, and who may need formal qualifications in order to realise their aspirations within, say, employment. In particular, for new learners overcoming what may be deep-seated anxieties about learning, recognition of achievement can be a critical factor in sustaining their commitment and building their confidence. The recording of achievement through summative assessment, especially if it is recognised through some kind of public examination, can be a transforming experience. Secondly, the organisations that provide learning, including colleges, community-based organisations, and training providers, need measures of success in order to support further progression of their

---

46   Taylor, 2002.
47   Black and Wiliam, 1998.

learners, for quality assurance and improvement systems, and to justify continued funding from LSCs and other funding bodies. Employers use learning outcomes as an indicator of the effectiveness of their staff training efforts, and often as a key criterion in the appointment and promotion of staff. In both cases, learning outcomes are being used as proxies for an assumed level of effectiveness in the workplace. Governmental arms-length agencies such as the national and local LSCs need to measure outcomes of learning to demonstrate their ability to achieve government targets, and in order to allocate resources strategically. Outcomes of learning are at the heart of the Common Inspection Framework used by Ofsted and the Adult Learning Inspectorate. Government departments, and units such as ABSSU, use measures of outcomes in learning to evaluate their strategic priorities, as part of the process of policy development, as measures of their success, and to justify their budget allocations to the Treasury.

We have seen that there are a number of different and overlapping ways in which the outcomes of learning can be identified or measured. However, in post-school education and training the product of all these processes is normally a qualification. The framework for funding and institutional performance measurement within post-school education in England and Wales is founded on the idea that learning leads to formal qualifications which are usually assessed externally. The assumption is that qualifications are the sole desired product of learning activity, for learners and for providers, agencies and government departments, and it is thus legitimate to use qualifications both for recognition of learning and for institutional performance measurement and funding. In many areas of post-school learning this may be a reasonable assumption, but for adult literacy, language and numeracy it is problematic for a number of reasons:

- Many learners, having had negative experiences at school, fear that a qualification-led learning regime will simply lead to a repetition of past failure: the system itself can act as a barrier to widening participation if it is perceived as one in which testing is the norm.

  Most learners did not want to take any exams and the overwhelming preference was for ongoing assessment ... some form of assessment to measure and recognise learning gain was valued but most learners preferred this to be an ongoing process based on discussion and portfolio building supported by tutor feedback and individual reflection ... people said they did not want to be exposed to the stress and pressure of tests and exams.[48]

- At level 1 and below, the qualifications themselves, however well-structured, are only useful for progression within further education: in the employment marketplace they are little more than formal evidence that learners have not achieved at GCSE-equivalent level, and thus could be used to discriminate against them. Many potential learners in the workplace, for example, might reasonably fear that signing up for a literacy learning programme would mark them out for possible redundancy.

---

48   Ward and Edwards, 2002.

- If funding and performance measurement depend on qualifications being achieved rather than on learning activity in general, there will be an inevitable tendency for providers to prefer learners who can achieve qualifications rather than those who can't or who prefer not to take external qualifications. At best, providers will focus on fitting their learners into the system of funding and performance measurement, rather than the other way round. At worst, there is ample evidence that a pressured and 'high stakes' environment including league tables of provider performance often leads to 'gaming' strategies designed to 'beat the system', an example of Goodhart's Law.[49]

- Any such distorting effects of particular assessment methods or the uses to which they are put, will be magnified in the context of learning in a number of 'bite-sized' chunks, as in that case 'summative assessment' is formally carried out more often. This applies to many adult learners of literacy, numeracy and language, most of whom learn part-time and whose programmes are typically made up of combinations of 'courses' treated bureaucratically as separate, and each of which has to record its own processes of assessment. This regulation is one of the difficulties facing curriculum managers trying to provide learning in 'bite-sized' chunks.

- The institutional and political emphasis on processes for measuring the outcomes of learning ignores the fact that for most adult literacy, language and numeracy learners, particularly those on short or small programmes, their achievements do not mark in any sense the end of the learning process: rather they are a platform for further learning and progression. The wider political significance of the measured outcomes tends to encourage teachers to focus more on the short-term qualification than on longer term and broader learning goals. Research shows that external tests, such as the British National Curriculum tests and the GCSEs, and indeed the National Basic Skills tests, which function as 'high-stakes' tests,[50] always dominate both teaching and assessment, and thus provide teachers with poor models for the more valuable formative assessment processes looked at in the next section of this paper.[51] Also:

  High stakes tests often result in a great deal of time being spent on practice tests, with test performance being highly valued and other achievements undervalued. Furthermore teachers' own assessments become mainly summative in function rather than formative.[52]

- Some methods used for summative assessment can have the effect of demotivating learners with low self-esteem and reducing the likelihood of further participation in learning:

  [Learners] who encounter difficulties and poor results are led to believe that they lack ability, and this belief leads them to attribute their difficulties to a defect in themselves about which they cannot do a great deal. So they 'retire hurt', avoid investing effort in learning which could only lead to disappointment, and try to build up their self-esteem in other ways.[53]

---

49   Perry, 2000; Wiliam, 2001.
50   Reder, 2002.
51   Black and Wiliam, 1998.
52   ARG, 2002.
53   Black and Wiliam, 1998.

None of these arguments imply that we should not be trying to measure the performance of provider institutions, or that we should not have sensible systems for allocating funding. Still less do they imply that we should not be using all available tools for assessing learners' achievements. We maintain rather that using the outcomes of summative assessment of learners for these broader and more politically charged purposes inevitably skews the process of teaching and learning by narrowing and concentrating its focus, and that this is particularly problematic and inappropriate for many adult learners of literacy, language and numeracy.

Following the development and research projects cited earlier in the paper, a consensus is now emerging over how to avoid these unintended outcomes and support students through a formative assessment approach based on learning objectives defined in Individual Learning Plans (ILPs), and how the same framework can be used if necessary for summative assessment. The approach, codified in Grief and Windsor 2002,[54] is being tested in practice across the country in the context of 'internally-accredited' literacy, language and numeracy programmes, and this exercise is being evaluated as part of the Planning Learning, Recording Achievement (PLRA) project, led by the LSDA and nearing completion. The approach is in essence not new: ILPs were a key feature of the Basic Skills Agency Quality Mark which was launched in 1992. The essential elements of this approach are:

- The learner commits to a period of learning and, following diagnostic assessment, takes part in the setting of their own learning goals for that period of learning.
- These learning goals are mapped to the national standards for adult literacy and/or numeracy.
- They can be set across a variety of levels and skills within the curriculum, so as to reflect the 'spiky profiles' of learners' abilities against the various elements of the national standards.
- They can differentiate between 'emerging', 'consolidating', and 'established' levels of attainment, reflecting terminology developed within the new national diagnostic assessment framework.
- The learning objectives on the ILP are used for developmental and reflexive formative assessment during the programme of learning: this can take a wide range of forms in practice.
- Summative assessment is carried out by using marked assignments and projects which are designed to demonstrate how far the learner has achieved their individual goals for the period of learning being assessed.
- As well as including progression advice and a clear indication of which learning goals have been achieved and which need more work, summative assessment formally provides data for the organisation and the funder on achievement, in the form of a document auditable against the provider's policy on assessment practice.

Standard quality assurance processes based on the Common Inspection Framework, including internal and perhaps external moderation of summative assessment

---

54   Grief and Windsor, 2002.

judgements and sampling of learners' work, are applied to ensure consistency and probity.

Similar processes have in fact been operating in many Basic Skills and Adult Community Learning programmes for some years. Achievement and retention data from internally accredited Basic Skills programmes have been routinely used for statistical and funding purposes since the beginning of the FEFC period, though the quality-assurance and audit processes were not as robust as they are now. Through development projects such as PLRA, these processes, systems, and model proformas are being piloted in relation to literacy, language and numeracy programmes for learners who do not wish to be assessed externally, mainly at Entry level. Similar processes have been piloted for adult community learning programmes,[55] and the first inspections of ACL within the Common Inspection Framework have tested them and found them resilient.[56]

Assessment for learning

Overall, the purpose of assessment is to improve standards, not merely to measure them.[57]

Assessment which is explicitly designed to promote learning is the single most powerful tool we have for both raising standards and empowering lifelong learners.[58]

Some assessment strategies encourage rote and superficial learning, they frequently have a negative impact and strategies are often used as a management tool, not as a system to discern learning needs.[59]

In the context of the previous discussion about the increasing political importance to teachers, provider organisations, LSCs and the government of achievement and retention data, it is sometimes forgotten that the most important function of assessment is to contribute to effective learning. NIACE, with Ofsted, believes that the value of assessment *for* learning in adult literacy, numeracy and language programmes should not be compromised by systems for assessment *of* learning. The purpose of this section of the paper is to suggest ways in which improvements to the present arrangements, based on this principle, would help learners, and support the national strategy.

NIACE believes that there are two ways in which present arrangements for assessment within adult literacy, numeracy and language should be improved in order to support more effective learning: firstly, by developing and supporting those features of the system for which there is strong evidence of positive effects on learning; and secondly, by removing those features of the assessment system for

---

55   Greenwood *et al.*, 2001.
56   E.g. ALI, 2003a; ALI, 2003b.
57   Ofsted, 1998.
58   ARG, 1999.
59   QCA, 2003.

which there is evidence that they reduce learning and damage learner motivation for the future.

As we have seen, for most learners of adult literacy, numeracy and language, it is not so much summative but 'sustainable' assessment that is needed.[60] For adult learners, and particularly those whose experience of education has been negative, developing the ability to assess their own learning effectively is an essential element of becoming fully self-directed. It is through the practice of formative assessment that teachers can help students develop these capacities. Formative assessment refers to 'all those activities undertaken by teachers and by their students assessing themselves, which provide information to be used as feedback to modify the teaching and learning activities in which they are engaged'.[61] The Black Box series of studies has found strong evidence that improving formative assessment raises standards, though it also stresses that this is not simple or a 'quick fix'.[62] These studies have found that effective formative assessment contributes to the development of self-esteem and willingness to take on educational challenges among learners; this chimes with the experience of adult literacy, numeracy and language teachers, that the more learners can consciously link their classroom activities with everyday literacy, numeracy and language practices, the more effective their learning is. In this view, formative assessment can help learners develop consciousness, reflectiveness and articulacy about their learning and their everyday practice, not just to improve the effectiveness of those practices, but as part of developing their capacity to learn in general. There is also evidence that improved formative assessment is particularly effective in raising the attainment of 'low-achieving' students and students with learning disabilities. NIACE would therefore like to see specific initiatives designed to support the development of explicit professional practice of formative assessment in adult literacy, numeracy and language learning. We suggest that this should be organised as a collaborative professional development process, as a way of disseminating and embedding the approach through the involvement of a wide range of practitioners.

However, we are not suggesting that such professional practice does not exist. Many teachers use formative assessment approaches systematically, others do so intuitively, and most others would if they were given professional development and support. However, a number of features of the present assessment system act as barriers to the further development and dissemination of this practice among teachers of adult literacy, numeracy and language. Some of them have been mentioned already: the heavy political and bureaucratic emphasis on summative assessment and measurable outcomes shifts attention from more developmental process-oriented aspects of learning, and this is aggravated by the tendency for adult learners to enrol for multiple short programmes, in each of which they are assessed separately. The radical differences between the assessment regimes for programmes at E3 and L1 are hard to explain in pedagogical terms, as is the exclusion of entry-level achievements from contributing to the national targets. We have already

---

60   Boud, 2000.
61   Black and Wiliam, 1998.
62   E.g. Black and Wiliam, 1998.

mentioned the evidence that tests, particularly if used as summative assessment tools, can demotivate learners, particularly those we most need to motivate and encourage. But the most significant problem in our view is the link between funding and performance measurement of provider organisations, and outcomes of learning as measured by this range of different methods. This situation is well-evidenced to produce a narrowing of the curriculum, prioritising summative over formative assessment, and 'teaching to the test':

> *By making the pressure on teachers and students to achieve good results on particular tests greater and greater, we can secure improvements in scores on those tests, but these improvements are secured at the expense of everything else. The tests, originally meant simply as a sample of the curriculum, come to be the whole curriculum.*[63]

Worse still, we are in danger of ensuring that the national targets for literacy and numeracy are met (as measured by the tests), but that this will not mean that standards have definitely improved, only that more people have been successfully taught to pass the tests.

NIACE believes that in order to support genuine improvements in adult literacy, numeracy and language attainment, the systems for assessing learners and those for allocating 'outcome' funding and measuring institutional performance *should be detached*. Assessment for learning cannot at the same time be assessment for college funding and for college performance. We believe that other less problematic indicators can be found to justify outcome-related funding, and that the infrastructure for quality assurance in post-16 providers is sufficiently robust to dispense with the raw achievement data. There are now embedded self-assessment procedures in most provider organisations, and these are backed up by the Common Inspection Framework, which is clear, accessible, and widely supported. It is therefore perverse to continue attaching so much political and economic significance to the raw data on the achievement of qualifications whose value in the market-place is at best equivocal.

Conclusions

This paper suggests that the present systems for measuring achievement in adult literacy, numeracy and language need to be made more coherent, consistent and transparent, in the interests of learners. It argues that the high-stakes significance of the outcomes of summative assessment of learning (funding, inspection, league tables, etc) is having unintended negative effects on the breadth and sustainability of learning itself, and calls for an end to the linkages between assessment of students' achievements, and assessment of providers' performance and funding. It draws

---

63   Wiliam, 2001.

attention to research suggesting that the most effective and practical way to improve learners' achievement is to improve the practice of formative assessment as part of teaching and learning, and calls for a shift in the priorities of the national strategy to reflect this.

This paper has not focussed in depth on the national tests for literacy and numeracy, but on the framework of which they are part. It does not argue that there is no role for standardised tests in adult literacy and numeracy: any assessment tool has its uses, provided it contributes to and does not inhibit learning. There is evidence that publishing the results of standardised tests can have a demotivating effect on learners with less confidence, because of the element of peer comparison. The logic of this is that testing can be more effective as a tool for formative assessment during learning, rather then as a means of summative assessment. This paper calls for research into these questions as a matter of urgency, and in fact, an LSDA programme has been investigating some of these issues during the past year.[64]

Finally, whatever imperfections there may be in the present arrangements for assessment and the measurement of achievement in adult literacy, numeracy and language, it is vitally important that learners' real achievements are recognised and celebrated within the system as it is at present. Since the Moser Report, there has been a high level of political will to tackle the problem of low basic skills. NIACE believes that it is essential to keep working to demonstrate the value of the resources that have been allocated to the national strategy, and that the simplest way to do this at the present time is to ensure that as many learners as possible are supported to gain the qualifications that count towards the national targets. NIACE will at the same time continue to argue for broadening the range of achievements that count towards the targets, as well as for other more structural improvements of the kind discussed in this paper.

Recommendations

- The national target for achievement should be propped up and enriched by a national target for participation.
- Achievements of literacy, numeracy and language learners at all levels should contribute to the national target.
- There should be more consistency in the summative assessment regulations for adult literacy, numeracy and language, particularly in relation to the E3–L1 transition.
- The confusing differences between the assessment requirements for Basic Skills and Key Skills should be simplified and improved, or removed altogether.
- Research and development should be implemented on approaches, techniques and tools that support assessment for learning.
- A toolkit on formative assessment in adult literacy, numeracy and language should

---

64   LSDA, 2002.

be produced: this production should be organised as a collaborative professional development activity.

- The 'Black Box' studies' findings, that using standardised tests for summative assessment can demotivate learners, should be investigated for adult learners of literacy, numeracy and language.

- Assessment for learning cannot at the same time be assessment for college funding and/or college performance: this link should be broken, and alternative methods of allocating outcome funding and measuring organisational performance found.

Acknowledgements

Thanks to Peter Lavender, Chris Taylor, Jan Eldred, Maurice Neville, who offered advice and comments at various points in the writing of this paper, and to Kate Moorse and Tim Oates who were very helpful with references, particularly to the Assessment Reform Group.

Jay Derrick

D'où venons-nous? Que sommes-nous? Où allons-nous?[65]

When in 1897 Gauguin completed 'D'où venons-nous? Que sommes-nous? Où allons-nous?' he considered it to be his masterpiece. Like much of his work the true meaning of this painting remains elusive. Certainly his interest in dreams, fantasy and symbolism demands much more than a literal translation. Even the title 'Where Do We Come From? What Are We? Where Are We Going?' appears to be in deliberate conflict with the arrangement of the images on this huge canvas. Only when the spectator learns that the artist requested that this work be 'read' from right to left does the vision of life as a journey from cradle to grave or from innocence to enlightenment become transparent (See back cover of this publication).

For those committed to delivery, the vision of lifelong learning and the relationship between policy and practice can seem equally opaque. In presenting this paper I have chosen to follow the sequence of Gauguin's visual rather than poetic language. In this respect the paper that follows begins with the end and ends with the beginning. I trust that this device gives readers a greater understanding of one of the key elements of the *Skills for Life* vision.

> *'The letter and the information it contained were both a relief and a surprise. At last I had impressed someone, they had confidence in me. They had offered me the job and wanted me to start a week on Monday but – there's always a but! – they wanted me to have completed my maths course and confirm my achievement with Personnel when I start. They didn't seem to mind when I said that my Maths wasn't too great and that I was attending a numeracy course; they seemed more pleased that I was looking to improve myself. What did she say: 'they wanted people with ambition and confidence'? Didn't recognise myself at first! I must let them know at the Centre that I'm ready and book an appointment for the test for next Monday. I'll ask for one about 10ish. I'll have got the kids off to school by then and calmed my nerves. Who'd have thought it: me calling the tune? Me telling them when I want to do the test? Me using a computer? Me pressing the button to say 'yes, I'm confident in these answers?' Me watching as my certificate is printed out? – Just like having your photograph taken really. Well, better get on and sort this out. Might as well*

---

65   Paul Gauguin: French, 1848–1903: 'Where Do We Come From? What Are We? Where Are We Going?' 1897, oil on canvas: 54 x 147 in (139.1 x 374.6 cm) Tompkins Collection, 1936 Museum of Fine Arts, Boston.

look at what to do next while I'm down at the Centre. I seem to remember
seeing something about a new on-line course on health and safety....'[66]

Preamble

Anyone who believes that *Skills for Life* has made its full impact, or judges current practices in the light of long-term policy imperatives, is missing the point. Equally, anyone who continues to measure or monitor the strategy in the light of *A Fresh Start*, Lord Moser's ground-breaking report on basic skills, has also failed to absorb the full intentions of the strategy and its role in supporting the government's broader economic and social policy agenda.

Skills for Life, along with *Success for All* and the *Skills Strategy*, are essential pillars of an agenda focussed on social inclusion and the democratisation of education and training. *Skills for Life* is this government's recognition of, and response to, the issues raised and recommendations made by Lord Moser. It was never intended as a low-cost or headline-grabbing attempt merely to address them. *Skills for Life* is an ambitious strategy. It has set out to change how we respond to and resolve the fundamental issues that have bedevilled adult education for many years. These are the issues of focus, participation, completion, achievement, quality, progression and the resources to deliver and secure them.

It is important to remember that there are still influential voices that believe that the greatest 'return' on educational investment is secured through spending on children and schools. Their thesis is that most of those beyond sixteen, and certainly those over nineteen, have had their opportunity and if they have chosen not to take their chances then they must take the consequences. Set against such views the government's commitment to adult learning is not just ambitious, it is also brave and generous. In the circumstances, who can deny ministers their right to measure a tangible return? That is, after all, what the targets have been designed to do.

The *Skills for Life* strategy has four interconnected themes: increasing demand, raising capacity, improving quality and increasing learner achievement. This interconnectedness is not just a theoretical construct: for those responsible for delivery it is real – a framework for action. Nevertheless, with such a disparate set of partners working across the full range of audiences and constituencies in a variety of different contexts and settings, it was always likely that, at least in the early stages, equal and even progress would not be secured across all themes. It was always likely that there would be some timelag in the strategy's development and implementation, and this has proved to be the case.

In Autumn 2001 the Adult Basic Skills Strategy Unit commissioned a thematic review of all further education provision from the Adult Learning Inspectorate (ALI) and the Office for Standards in Education (Ofsted). Published in September 2003, the review reported on provision between 1 April 2002 and 31 May 2003. Entitled *Literacy, numeracy and English for speakers of other languages: a survey of current*

---

66   History, Reality or Fantasy – A Personal Reflection on Assessment within *Skills for Life: the national strategy for improving adult literacy and numeracy* (DfES, 2001).

practice in post-16 and adult provision it has provided early and timely confirmation of this lag.

In the review's main findings, under the heading 'Achievement and standards', the inspectorates report that 'The Skills for Life initiative has been successful in rapidly increasing the number of learners on literacy, numeracy and ESOL courses.' However, under 'Quality of education and training' they go on to say that:

> *There is a shortage of teaching expertise in literacy and numeracy in all sectors, but particularly in Jobcentre Plus provision, work-based learning for young people, in prison education and in learndirect provision. There is a severe shortage of ESOL tutors in London.*[67]

Since the launch of the strategy in March 2001 successive government ministers have recognised that establishing and securing a balance between 'quality' and 'widening participation' would be difficult. Nevertheless, in successive speeches they have reinforced their recognition of the scale of the challenge and their commitment to addressing it. Their message has been consistent and clear, 'After decades of neglect there can be no quick fix, this government is in it for the long haul.'

'Neglect' is quite a harsh description to accept, especially if you are one of the many individuals who, during these decades, have given freely of their time, commitment and dedication, and who have worked to improve the lot of those adults with the lowest levels of literacy, language and numeracy. Written off by others, these adult learners are quick to accept the blame for their weaknesses and express this through anger, despondency or frustration. As a consequence, adult basic skills teachers have often become their champions, their guardians and their protectors. To compound the problem, these teachers, working with some of the most challenging of learners, have themselves often been marginalised within their sector. They have suffered from limited resources, usually poor teaching accommodation, often with the worst conditions of service, tenure and access to training, and the limited career and progression opportunities these brought. 'Neglect' in such circumstances has meant the failure of successive governments to invest in the sector and the failure of providers to invest in their curriculum resources, their teachers and their learners.

The *Skills for Life* strategy is evidence that the government will no longer neglect the sector. Through the Learning and Skills Council, providers have been given the incentives to get to grips with the full range of learner needs, while the Adult Learning Inspectorate and Ofsted have the drivers and the levers to engage with the attitudes and performance of providers.

Now that these barriers have been identified and dismantled, the full scale of the challenge is evident and our capacity and our collective preparedness, to overcome this neglect are being put to the test.

---

67   ALI/Ofsted, 2003.

Où allons-nous?[68]

Please suspend your disbelief: imagine that a point is eventually reached where...

- Individuals are not stigmatised by the fact that they do not have the English or mathematics skills necessary to take a full part in society, be it at home, at work or within their communities.
- People openly discuss their strengths and weaknesses, what they know or don't know, and have a desire to be as good as they can be and a determination as well as an opportunity to do something about it.
- This enlightened state means that they are true lifelong learners, ready and able to continue their learning journey at a pace which suits their individual needs and no matter how long it takes.
- Access is straightforward, and a variety of local organisations provide individual advice and guidance. The information and support they give starts from where the learner is, looks at what their aims and aspirations are, what knowledge and skills they already possess, and discusses how best to move them forward. Alternative routes are offered and discussed, and a pathway decided upon.
- Before entry to a programme, everyone is screened to see whether they have the appropriate skills to enable them to take full advantage of their programme of learning. This screening is not onerous; it is straightforward, quick and without stigma. Because it is part of the enrolment process and, as it focusses on learners' needs, is undertaken in a way that matches their experience and leads to learning which is free, no-one objects to participating in the process.
- Those whose essential skills in English, mathematics or ICT need to be addressed take an initial assessment before they start the course. This helps the teacher identify the level of skills support they need and whether the embedded approach to learning will be sufficient or whether they need some additional learning support to help them take full advantage of their main programme of studies.
- Once placed, all learners undergo a diagnostic assessment that looks at their individual strengths and weaknesses and contributes to the creation of an individual learning plan (ILP). This plan will set out each learner's aims and aspirations as well as what they need to do to achieve them. These ILPs are theirs; they own them, believe in them, and use them as a contract between themselves and their teachers.
- All learners recognise the importance of qualifications. As well as being a symbol of their achievement to themselves, their friends and families, they have credibility and currency. There is no mystery associated with them, and learners know that they will not be entered for them unless or until they are ready. The individual is as much in control of the assessment process as the learning process. This is a partnership between teacher and learner and between learner and learner. In a society that truly values lifelong education, everyone is both a teacher and a learner.

---

68   Where are we going?

- Programmes are delivered by fully qualified teachers whose dedication and enthusiasm are matched by their capability and confidence in themselves, their organisation and the further and adult education sector as a whole. Some learners develop their skills embedded within vocational programmes and the learning is led by vocational experts who are aware of, and able to meet, the literacy, language and numeracy needs of their learners. In some circumstances, these experts are assisted by qualified literacy, language or numeracy support staff.

- Throughout the learning process the touchstone of progress is the ILP; routines are established that empower learners to discuss their progress, take responsibility for reviewing and revising their ILP in the light of their achievements and determine which qualifications best meet their immediate, medium and long-term needs.

- There is a genuine recognition that all lifelong learners should have a nationally recognised qualification in English, mathematics and ICT, and all learners are encouraged to select a qualification and assessment regime that is appropriate to their current level of skill as well as to plan and prepare for higher levels and more challenging assessment.

- The confusion that once existed between National Certificates in Literacy, Numeracy and ESOL and Key Skills has been resolved, and all teachers, as a result of their training, now recognise that for assessment and qualifications to be fit for purpose, they must be built into delivery and practice and that access to a national qualification is both an entitlement and a requirement. Also, qualification developers and regulators have overcome their lack of trust in the reliability of technology, and ICT-based assessment. E-assessment is now seen to be as valid a method as observed and paper-based approaches. The new unitised framework also benefits from the reform of 14–19 education; literacy and numeracy are recognised as essential components of English and mathematics capability, thus increasing coherence across the ages and stages of education and training as well as finally eliminating any concerns about credibility and validity.

- The introduction of ICT-based assessment has revolutionised assessment procedures and processes, and now provides teachers and learners with the type of information that enables the partnership to address weaknesses and build on strengths. ICT-based assessment eliminates the historical tensions between assessment *for* and assessment *of* learning. Feedback can be as detailed as desired and can range from the simple right and wrong, to the accuracy level in specific aspects of the subject, as well as checking the learners' confidence in certain areas by recording how long it takes to respond accurately to specific questions or the number of times an answer was changed. Data can also be made available at an individual, group, age or skill level to enable comparisons to be made.

- The increased autonomy of the learner is also reflected in the breadth of coverage of assessment as well as the increased flexibility and access demanded. The use of ICT-based technology means that more of the standards and content of the curriculum can be assessed. ICT-based assessment is able to assess an ever-widening range of skills. In literacy, listening skills, as well as the ability to generate text, can be assessed. In numeracy, the ability to mathematise information and solve problems can also be explored and analysed.

- Flexibility of access, that is assessment at a time, in a place and at a pace most appropriate to the learner, is widely available. This ease of access enables the full range of contexts and settings to match the delivery of provision and the needs of the learners with the form of assessment for each individual or group; on site, on demand, and on-line. The particular rhythms of audiences and constituencies – be they in general Further Education Colleges, Adult and Community Learning Centres or the workplace – are addressed.

When this approach to learning and assessment is delivered, the current arguments against change will be shown to be groundless, and the resistance of those who see themselves as protecting the learners will be shown to be what it is: motivated by self-interest and a desire to stagnate rather than progress and improve.

I have never yet met a learner who, once empowered, didn't want to join the real world: get a qualification, get a job, get a life – usually one better than the one they already have. The *Skills for Life* strategy has this as its greatest aspiration: one that is already available to some but must be delivered to all.

Que sommes-nous?[69]

Having shared the vision with you, there is no need to ask you to suspend your disbelief further: we now move to our experience of the present.

In September 2003 the Executive Summary of the ALI/Ofsted thematic review gave everyone a snapshot of the early impact of the *Skills for Life* strategy:

> *The Skills for Life initiative has been highly successful in increasing the number of literacy, numeracy and ESOL learners and in raising the profile of this area of learning, but there needs to be a sharper focus on the quality of the education and training that is available. Few providers, other than the best colleges, are monitoring retention and achievement rates or measuring the effectiveness of their learning support.*[70]

At the time this implied failure to deliver on quality offended sensibilities and challenged beliefs. Further, it failed to accord with many experiences of the progress made by *Skills for Life* to date. The touchstone of the strategy has been a focus on improving quality and equality of access to all learners. In Autumn 2002 in the introduction to 'Success in Adult Literacy, Numeracy and ESOL Provision' I wrote the following words on provision and entitlement:

---

69   What are we?
70   ALI/Ofsted, 2003.

… all adult learning in literacy, numeracy and ESOL will be underpinned by:

* *the national standards for literacy and numeracy at Entry level, level 1 and level 2;*

* *the core curricula for literacy, numeracy and ESOL, with a curriculum framework for Learners with Learning Difficulties and/or Disabilities;*
* *a common screening tool; and*
* *appropriate diagnostic assessment.*

This means that every adult learner can expect to have free access to:

* *impartial advice and guidance on how to improve their skills;*
* *a confidential report based on a diagnostic assessment which identifies their strengths and weaknesses in literacy, language and numeracy;*
* *an individual learning plan that identifies realistic milestones and targets;*
* *a relevant programme of learning which has been developed using the national standards that matches their aims and aspirations to their current abilities and future potential;*
* *ongoing feedback and support that is clear, meaningful and motivating;*
* *nationally recognised qualifications that are valued by employers; and*
* *timely information and encouragement to help proactive progression to other education, training or employment opportunities.*

This means that all providers, irrespective of audience, context or setting, must:

* *prepare and undertake an annual self-assessment that informs their plans to address weaknesses and secure continuous improvement*
* *monitor, recognise and record all learner progress through non-externally accredited achievement as well as through national qualifications;*
* *raise the level of competence of all teachers of literacy, numeracy and ESOL by offering opportunities for continuous professional development and access to programmes of training that lead to nationally recognised qualifications.*[71]

We know that, thankfully, this is the experience of increasing numbers of learners because the inspection grades and the LSC provider reviews tell us so. Unfortunately, the ALI/Ofsted thematic review also sets out clearly that this is not the case for many

---

71   DfES, 2002.

of these learners. The debate over assessment *of* learning through qualifications and other measures of achievement and assessment *for* learning becomes little more than one of semantics when we read that:

> *Weaknesses in initial assessment and the poor quality of most individual learning plans (ILPs) mean that it is difficult to assess the progress of individual learners, especially those who are not working towards external accreditation.*[72]

Equally, the celebration of different approaches to delivery and the importance of embedding become meaningless when we read that, in some provision, learning support has become little more than amanuensis for the completion of portfolio-based qualifications.

> *Inexperienced support tutors often focus on completing the assignments and tasks at the expense of developing the learners' understanding and skills. They look up words in the dictionary rather than show the learner how to do it....Often they are so intent on making speedy progress that they answer their own questions before the learner has had time to think.*[73]

It is less than three years since the Prime Minister launched the *Skills for Life* strategy and the ALI/Ofsted review only reports on the unevenness of its early impact over the first two years, so we should not be too disheartened. None the less, for those committed to changing the culture and making an immediate difference the report does make depressing reading in places:

> *Many of the learners with the greatest need are with providers with the least qualified staff, the fewest resources and the lowest budget for staff training.*[74]

Those who have heard me speak on the strategy will know my view that in *Skills for Life* we are all learners. The cast list is long and varied: we may be learners seeking to improve our literacy, language or numeracy skills; teachers seeking to help learners improve their literacy, language and numeracy skills; trainers seeking to train the teachers who help learners to improve their literacy, language and numeracy skills; funding agencies seeking to resource the trainers who train the teachers who help the learners to improve their literacy, language and numeracy skills; or the policy makers seeking to develop the strategy for the funding agencies who resource the trainers who train the teachers who help the learners to improve their literacy, language and numeracy skills.

Given the findings in the thematic review, we still have a lot to learn – apart, that is, from those centres of excellence who are in the vanguard of delivery and who have shown themselves well able to increase demand while at the same time securing

---

72   ALI/Ofsted 2003.
73   ALI/Ofsted, 2003.
74   ALI/Ofsted, 2003.

quality. Even in identifying the number of learners in the system there is a degree of uncertainty because not all learning is managed by LSC-approved providers, and without a discrete learner-identification system reliable data is not yet available. That said, work is being undertaken on this and the quality of data is increasingly reliable and robust. The figures below represent the most up-to-date record of the number of learners in the system for LSC-funded provision:

April 2001–July 2004: Number of learning opportunities = 4.3 million
Number of individual learners = 1.9 million[75]

The ALI/Ofsted thematic review itself is not always precisely focused in its criticisms. I believe it is inappropriate to criticise the sector for its lack of qualified teachers when the first suitable qualifications were only approved by the Qualifications and Curriculum Authority (QCA) and the associated programmes endorsed by Further Education National Training Organisation (FENTO) in September 2002 – mid-way through the review period. Nor should we be unreasonably crtical of certain contexts and settings for their poor performance when this has been the first time that they have ever had their literacy, language or numeracy provision reported upon separately.

The picture painted by the thematic review is not one of unqualified success, but one thing is clear from the findings: the Inspectorates do support the ambitions of the strategy and all its components, including the qualifications. Indeed, one of the notable features of the review is the positive light in which qualifications are shown in respect of monitoring the use of the ILP and increasing retention rates.

Contrary to the concerns of some commentators, at no point do the findings suggest that people are teaching towards the test, distorting delivery to meet the needs of the targets or putting qualifications above the needs of the learners. Indeed, the opposite seems to be the case: the inspectorates contend that the failure to link funding to qualifications is at least in part responsible for programmes of poor quality:

On discrete literacy, numeracy and language courses in colleges, funding is no longer dependent on the learners working towards external accreditation and, in many colleges, there are few learners who are preparing for an external examination. Some providers, particularly of New Deal, 25+ and work-based learning for adults, are not offering learners the opportunity to take qualifications in literacy, numeracy and language, although they would benefit from doing so.[76]

This is probably the best place to address the current link between the targets and funding. The first point to make is that the Public Service Agreements (PSAs) with the Treasury do not drive the *Skills for Life* strategy; they actually fuel it. The

---

75   LSC figures for the period, which include some projections for 2004.
76   ALI/Ofsted, 2003.

strategy has been framed and resourced so that every learner has an entitlement to free adult literacy, language and numeracy provision offered by recognised and approved providers from pre-entry level up to and including Level 2. There is no cap on the length of time taken nor is there a specified requirement for a nationally recognised qualification. As long as the learner meets the achievements as set out in the ILR and the programme is underpinned by the appropriate national standards in literacy and numeracy, the provider has full access to the 1.4 weighting, the disadvantaged uplift and the achievement funding. This is available whether the learner's learning outcomes contribute to the national targets or not. Reflecting further on the data I provided earlier on LSC-funded provision:

> *between April and July 2003 there were at least 3.09 million learning opportunities taken by 1.9 million individual learners.*
>
> *During this period the milestone of 470,000 achievements that count towards the target was met. In respect of the target an individual's achievements only count once, even though they may gain several qualifications through a range of levels and across literacy, language and numeracy skills. In this context an additional 193,000 national qualifications were achieved that did not count towards the target.*[77]

Of course, data can be manipulated: the above figures could be interpreted to suggest that:

- There are many learners in the system who are attempting but failing to achieve national qualifications.
- There are many learners in the system who are not ready to access national qualifications; they need longer learning time.
- There are many learners who are not interested in accessing national qualifications.
- There are many learners who are not being given access to national qualifications.

Each of the above factors (and probably others not listed) contributes to the reality. However, the picture that is emerging is not a consistent one. In respect of the national qualifications at entry level, level 1 and level 2 some organisations have shown their faith in the system and have committed those learners who are ready to sit the tests or submit the portfolio, depending on the assessment vehicle used. Other organisations make virtually no use of nationally recognised measures of achievement. I have been told of one college of further education that is drawing down over £4 million of LSC funding to support *Skills for Life* provision and currently provides minimal access for learners to nationally recognised qualifications, thereby making little or no contribution to the target at all.

Other colleges have done the sums, looked at the risks and calculated that if they enter candidates for nationally recognised qualifications they will incur costs for:

---

77   LSC figures for the period which include some projections for 2003.

- qualification registration
- qualification administration
- the use of valuable accommodation for assessments.

There is also no guarantee their learners will achieve success in a national qualification, whilst if they use their own internal system of certification none of these costs applies and they can 'manage' the internal achievement process effectively and efficiently.

Where is the learner in all of this? In a system where, according to a recent UfI/learndirect survey, over 90 per cent of learners said they would take the advice of their teachers in deciding what to study, what qualification to sit and when to sit for it, the roles of the teacher and the learning provider are crucial. Against such inequalities in the approach to assessment and to recognised qualifications, is it surprising that the LSC is beginning to reflect on the appropriateness and equity of the current funding mechanism? To date, the inspection findings and other information in no way suggest that the funding method as it stands is skewing delivery towards the targets. In fact the altruism that underpinned the LSC's negotiations with the DfES on the current funding method has actually resulted in some quarters in the very opposite.

Before I leave the question of targets, it is worth reflecting on the proposal that what we need is more, not fewer, targets. It is suggested that we have targets for:

- participation, to stimulate widening participation and increasing engagement
- all of a learner's qualification, irrespective of skill or level
- achievement of entry levels 1 and 2 qualifications.

I am not persuaded by these suggestions, in part because they are based on a misunderstanding of the role of the PSA targets, who needs to know about them, what they are designed to do, and what the outcome of such an increase in the number of targets is likely to be.

There is no need for a participation target because we can already obtain this data from the LSC, without it needing to be 'target driven'. Also, as I suggested earlier, those who look to interpret data to serve their own ideological positions are unlikely to share a common interpretation of the territory. They will focus on the conversion factors from participation to achievement. A simple quantitative approach must ignore the nuances and subtleties of individual learning, spiky profiles[78] and the learner-centred approach, especially when it may take one learner a year to make the progress that another may make in a month. The multiple counting of achievements and the inclusion of entry levels 1 and 2 are essentially redundant for the same reasons. They could all be counted, but we would have to renegotiate the target figures upwards to include these achievements, thereby increasing the pressure on organisations, teachers and learners. Another misunderstanding here is that an Entry 1 or 2 achievement or a further qualification at level 1 or 2 is without value. It

---

78   I first used this term in 2000, when the National Standards were being developed, in an attempt to describe the uneven nature of an adult's level of competence and development.

certainly may be for the narrow purpose of accumulating numbers for the 'target', but it is not for the learner.

If learners are at the heart of everything we do we should do nothing that jeopardises their opportunities. The LSC has never said it will not fund further qualifications or those below Entry 3. As I have shown earlier, the risk to the current funding regime is from those who use the funding method's flexibility to access the available resource and deny those learners who are capable and confident access to any national qualifications.

The argument, of course, is that high-quality learning is most important, and certainly more important than national qualifications that lack credibility because they do not cover all of the standards, are based on a fixed-response format, and are not recognised by employers.

The history of the national qualifications in literacy, numeracy and ESOL will be explored later in this paper, but at this point it is important to note that their development was underpinned by the following tenets:

- to enable learners to access testing on demand – any time, any place, anywhere
- to use forms of assessment that matched the type of knowledge, skill or understanding being assessed
- to ensure that the assessment was accessible, manageable, reliable and meaningful
- to develop a system capable of addressing the needs of a mass entry
- to prepare for new developments, including the use of ICT and the unitisation of qualifications
- to bring clarity, coherence and consistency to the parallel developments and review of key skills.

On reflection, tremendous progress has been made in all but one essential area – the effective communication of this key element of the teaching and learning infrastructure. I am concerned when I continue to read that teachers are desperate for a literacy qualification that does more than assess document and prose literacy, that there is no role for problem-solving in the numeracy test, or that people are confused about the relationship between the Key Skills of Communication and Application of Number and the basic skills of literacy and numeracy.

A related issue is why the Entry-level qualifications for both skills cover all of the standards but the level 1 and 2 certificates do not. The answer to these concerns has been set out many times before and I will set it out again here for the sake of clarity.

The external assessment tests for the Key Skills of Communication and Application of Number at levels 1 and 2 and the national tests in literacy and numeracy at the corresponding level are identical. These tests were designed to confirm that learners at these levels had the underpinning skills necessary to apply them in a context that was meaningful and motivating to them. Given how diverse these contexts and settings are, the portfolio approach set out in the Key Skill was seen as the most accessible and relevant approach to the assessment of this application. The model recommended and agreed[79] consists of the external Key Skill

---

79   The Technical Implementation Group (TIG) created by Baroness Blackstone.

assessment or the national test combined with the Key Skill portfolio. This model provides full coverage of the national standards and avoids confusing the learners by creating competing qualifications. There is no need to have a similar approach at Entry level because there are no Key Skills at entry level. This relationship between the Key Skills specifications and the National Literacy and Numeracy Standards and their assessment has been signalled whenever and wherever an opportunity has arisen. For example in QCA's original guidance on the National Standards published in August 2000 there is a section entitled 'The standards and the key skills specifications'. Under the sub heading 'The links between the skills' it says:

> *The standards relate most directly to Part A of the key skills units of communication and application of number at levels 1 and 2. The standards for literacy and numeracy specify the skills and capabilities for each skill at each level. In this way they provide the amplification of the knowledge, techniques and understanding described in Part A of the key skills units at the equivalent level.*
>
> *The alignment provides key skills practitioners with an opportunity to confirm that learners possess the range of knowledge, techniques and understanding appropriate for the key skill unit and its level.*
>
> *The relationship of the standards to the key skill units also supports curriculum and qualification developers seeking to secure consistency and coherence for learners.*
>
> *Opportunities should be created for the functionally literate adult to become an effective communicator and for the numerate adult to become confident and capable of applying number in a variety of contexts.*[80]

From these clear statements the relationship between the new National Certificates and Key Skills qualifications was developed. The test is used as an assessment instrument at levels 1 and 2 because it was necessary to bring greater rigour and reliability to the assessment of key skills. In the case of literacy and numeracy (soon to include ESOL), this approach is designed to bring the qualifications in to the mainstream by using an approach appropriate for qualifications at this level of demand. Test instruments were not generally encouraged for assessment at Entry level because this was where the most vulnerable and under-confident learners are to be found. At Entry level a careful balance was struck between engagement and inclusion as against rigour and reliability and for that reason a portfolio approach was seen as the most appropriate.

At levels 1 and 2 the use of an assessment instrument that used fixed-response questions was chosen for a multiplicity of reasons but essentially to ensure increase in access and flexibility of assessment. The use of fixed-response tests facilitated the use of machine marking and the development of a format capable of being transferred to on-screen, on-line assessment through ICT. Another key consideration was the impact on the qualification of a mass uptake and the availability of experts capable of acting as markers. It was important that the new qualification did not stall

---

80   QCA, 2000.

through the lack of experienced markers. This decision should be evaluated against the chaos that surrounded the introduction of the Curriculum 2000 reforms and the disastrous impact that the shortage of markers has had on the credibility of some of these reforms and the currency of the new 'A' levels, not to mention the unnecessary suffering and uncertainties this created for candidates. In such a context I believe the decision has proved to be both accurate and appropriate. While there have been trade-offs in coverage for those who have recognised the potential of progression through the levels of literacy and numeracy to GCSEs and vocational qualifications or transition from a national certificate to a full key skill qualification, the benefits have been tangible and all aspects of the learning, meaningful.

My response to those who are concerned about the limiting nature of the national certificates, or who are desperate to ensure that teaching to the qualification does not limit the learner's horizons, is obvious and straightforward. Adopt the key skills approach, teach to the key skill and cover the full set of standards. Use the unitised approach by accessing the test as soon as the learner is confident. The argument that this is yet another exam just like at school is not sustainable. There has never been a test like this in school[81] and it looks like no examination an adult learner will have seen before. This was never designed as an 'end test'; it was designed to be used when a learner is ready. The achievement of a national certificate in literacy or numeracy, whilst potentially an end in itself, should not be seen as this. It is a milestone on a learning journey. For many, it will be the springboard for more challenging programmes or qualifications, for others it will give them the confidence to be more positive in their everyday activities at home or at work.

The use of machine marking by awarding bodies has enabled these qualifications to break new ground in confirming and reporting results. Tests that originally could be sat only twice a year are now regularly available at least once a month in every context, with some providers being able to access them weekly, and others on demand. Awarding and reporting, which once took several months, are now being achieved in days by some awarding bodies. Once the only information on a learner's performance was 'pass' or 'fail', teachers are now being provided with increasingly detailed feedback on performance. The use of ICT has already resulted in some learners being told how they have done immediately, at the push of a button.

The assessment of literacy and numeracy is in the vanguard of assessment research and development. Like the targets, this is of little or no consequence to the learner but should mean a great deal to teachers of literacy, language and numeracy and who for so long have been perceived as occupying the margins of education and training. The *Skills for Life* strategy and those who deliver it are beginning to set the education and training agenda for adult learning and achievement and this means achievement in its widest and most inclusive sense.

Earlier, I attempted to separate out targets from qualification achievements. It is also important to remember that while all achievements are not qualifications, all qualifications are achievements. I was also critical of those organisations that sought to take advantage of achievement funding without the risk of losing it by seeking qualification outcomes. I remain committed to ensuring that in a learner-centred

---

81   This is no longer the case as the national certificates were added to the Section 96 list in November 2003.

approach any and all achievements should be recognised and celebrated. That is why the Adult Basic Skills Strategy Unit has invested so much in partnership with the LSC in projects such as the Planning Learning and Recording Achievement (PLRs)[82] and commissioning and funding NIACE's Regional Achievement Programme (RAP). As with the literacy and numeracy qualifications described above, these non-externally-accredited achievements are the milestones or stepping stones that mark and assist progress in achieving national qualifications and encourage the learner to take the next step on their learning journey. The risk is that in over-stating the relevance or status of these stepping-stone achievements we are drawn back to past practice when adults' basic skills and qualifications in literacy, language or numeracy received no recognition, no status and were seen as having no strategic role to play in lifelong learning.

D'où venons-nous?[83]

The history of basic skills is littered with many 'false dawns' where short-term funding has promised much and delivered little in respect of mainstream, sustained provision. What progress there has been has come in spite of successive governments' lack of provision of adequate and effective resources. That any progress has been possible in such an unsupportive environment is the result of the enthusiasm and dedication of those working in the sector, and the encouragement and support received from key agencies such as the Basic Skills Agency.

In April 1998 the Further Education Funding Council's Inspectorate published a Curriculum Area Survey Report on Basic Education. In its Summary the report noted that this area addresses some 231,700 learners in general further education colleges, plus a further 70,500 in external institutions. Also, its key finding that '*A common feature of the less effective provision is that the needs of the learners are not adequately assessed and met*' is uncomfortably familiar.

In its Conclusions the report set out an agenda for action which was embraced in its entirety by *A Fresh Start* and later embedded within the *Skills for Life* strategy:

> *In order to improve the quality of provision in this programme area, colleges should address the following issues:*
> * *the comparatively low standards in the programme area*
> * *inadequate curriculum guidance for teachers and insufficient sharing of good practice*
> * *ineffective assessment of learners' needs in many colleges*
> * *much teaching which fails to meet the needs of learners, particularly those with learning difficulties and disabilities*
> * *lower rates of achievement than in other programme areas*

---

82   The Adult Basic Skills Strategy Unit funded this project jointly with the LSC in 2002–03.

83   Where do we come from?

* *inappropriate forms of accreditation for programmes followed by many students*
* *the lack of planned progression for many students*
* *the ineffective collection and use of management information*
* *the lack of sufficiently rigorous arrangements for assuring quality*
* *inadequate staff development and management support, especially for the growing number of part time teachers*
* *the under use of information technology as a learning resource.*[84]

The findings of this report reflect the traditionally low levels of investment in adult learning which began to 'bite' in the 1980s. Like most adult education, literacy and numeracy provision was underdeveloped, underfunded and undervalued. Dedicated teachers, usually without secure contracts, resources or status, worked with enthusiastic volunteers to make a difference. Where teachers were well led, managed and trained, and understood learners' needs, basic skills were embedded as part of the adult provision. Where leadership, management and training was not seen as a priority, basic skills provision became marginalised, invisible or disappeared altogether. For some providers, outreach was a means of widening participation and integration. For others, it was a way of maintaining a discreet distance from mainstream provision. Much of the development funding was provided by special projects, local initiatives and occasionally the European Social Fund, all of which only offered short-term, pump-priming resources. Basic skills relied on projects and short-term initiatives, sustainability and mainstreaming were words hardly ever used or discussed.

As this adult provision was not part of the mainstream there was no relationship established with new initiatives in general, and in particular none with vocational education and training designed to increase the generic skills of young people and the workforce. Opportunities were missed to link the partner skills of literacy and communication or numeracy and application of number. Lord Dearing's post-compulsory world of education and training saw key skills (core skills) become a required part of General National Vocational Qualifications (GNVQs) and National Vocational Qualifications (NVQs). These skills were recognised by employers as being essential. Employers complained that young people leaving school with GCSEs in English and mathematics could not answer the telephone, write a letter or measure a length of wood accurately (unfortunately, some still are complaining!). The problem was that because these GNVQs and NVQs focussed on performance and competence in the vocational arena, few thought it important to teach the underpinning skills that were essential to speaking, reading, writing or measuring (unfortunately, many still don't!).

The review of Key Skills ordered by Baroness Blackstone asked the QCA to introduce external assessment to in order to restore some credibility to these qualifications and to make sure that they did what they claimed to do: confirm that young people actually could communicate effectively and calculate accurately. It is

---

84   FEFC, 1998.

worth noting here that before the review young people were obtaining their qualifications in enormous numbers yet employers were continuing to complain about the lack of key skills in new entrants to the workplace. In 1999 awarding-body figures suggested that less than 3 per cent of those who failed a GNVQ did so because of their key skills. What we had were high levels of achievement but apparently little applied learning or competence. As a result the credibility of Key Skills was threatened.

The analysis of the situation resulted in a decision to bring together the adult basic skills agenda, as highlighted by Lord Moser's work, and the introduction of new key skills qualifications by the QCA. The Key Skills Pilot's recommendations were brought together with the recommendations of *A Fresh Start*. Lord Moser recommended that the achievement of a basic skill in literacy or numeracy should be a prerequisite for an achievement of the Key Skill in communication or application of number. In response QCA embedded literacy and numeracy assessment within the new Key Skills Assessment Model. At the time this approach was seen by ministers as very persuasive and very logical: Lord Moser's committee and Baroness Blackstone's Technical Implementation Group recognised that if a learner did not have the basic knowledge, skills and understanding, they could not independently select and apply their skills effectively and efficiently in any context.

In order that this policy alignment was coherent with technical developments, the new standards in literacy and numeracy were triangulated with the appropriate Key Skill specification and its levels, the key stages of the National Curriculum and equivalent components of the GCSEs in English and mathematics. This technical alignment was embedded even further when DfES Ministers took QCA's advice to develop common tests for the new qualifications in literacy and numeracy and those for communication and application of number at levels 1 and 2.

The 'assessment development' for Key Skills had begun as early as 1997 and was a challenging and tortuous process, beginning with a Ministerial requirement for a twenty-hour assignment for each skill at each level. These assignments were to be externally set, internally marked and externally moderated. Again the theory seemed appropriate; enable teachers to build key skills assessment into their existing delivery. However, such an approach proved impractical because of the pressure it placed on learning and learners, the time it took for teachers to mark and the development costs it placed initially on awarding bodies transferred eventually back to centres and ultimately the public purse. Developers worked with the tensions facing any assessment instrument, balancing reliability (which awarding bodies required) with manageability (which teachers required) with authenticity (which learners deserved).

The model that emerged as a solution to these tensions is the one described in my section 'Where are we going?'. However, it was recognised that by September 1999, the scheduled launch date for the key skills qualification, this reliable and robust regime would not be available. An interim model described in 'Where are we?' was agreed. The DfES promised QCA substantial funding to develop and deliver the aspirational model. The scheduled launch date was delayed until September 2000 to enable all the government's post-16 reforms to be introduced together as Curriculum 2000. Those pilot centres and others who had prepared for the new key skills arrangements had access to a limited assessment regime as part of what was described as a 'Phased Implementation'.

Awarding bodies that delivered their own basic skills qualifications were put on notice that these were to be phased out between 1999 and August 2001. As from September 2001 only new entry level qualifications that met the QCA guidelines and the tests developed centrally by QCA at levels 1 and 2 for the key skills would be available as the new national certificates in literacy and numeracy. As might be imagined this new development was not universally popular among awarding bodies because it undermined their independence and market share. However, given the FEFC Inspectorate's comments on the chaotic nature of the existing qualifications, the need for credibility and the increased status of literacy and numeracy and, of course, the departments' commitment to investing substantially in development costs, all awarding bodies agreed to the principle and the practice. Thus for the first time in England there was a national qualification that everyone – irrespective of who they were, where they lived, where they learned or which awarding body their organisation used – would have the opportunity to access: a qualification that was identical in every way. This was a major development and has underpinned the *Skills for Life* strategy by securing coherence in the key area of achievement. The move also established that in delivering the strategy partnership was in this instance more important than competition.

The national awarding bodies, in particular City and Guilds, Edexcel and OCR, showed tremendous commitment to the strategy at this point and their ongoing support from then on should be both acknowledged and celebrated. Indeed, in the four years since the DfES agreed the assessment policy arrangements for key skills and literacy and numeracy it has been the awarding bodies that have taken every opportunity to move the agenda forward and I have little doubt that it will be they, with the guidance and support of QCA, who will deliver the vision as set out in summer 1999.

On reflection

Many years ago I worked as a manager in adult education for a local authority that prided itself as having the largest adult education provision in England. In my first meeting with my new line manager I was asked the question, 'Well Barry, how do you feel: optimistic or pessimistic?' For those of you who remember the challenges facing adult education in the mid 1980s, these words may have a chilling resonance. My immediate reply was, 'Neither – I'm realistic'. This realism continues to underpin all of my professional practice but my optimism for the future remains undiminished.

I take it as an honour and a privilege that I have had some responsibility for delivering the *Skills for Life* strategy in a form, at a pace and at a cost that is manageable, relevant and realistic. From the outset I recognised that the assessment regime that we were putting in place could only at best be an interim approach designed to move us forward in a meaningful and constructive way. My intention, originally at the National Council for Vocational Qualifications, followed by the QCA and more recently at the DfES, has been to ensure that what has been introduced is capable of development, progression and of being responsive to the changing needs of learners as well as policy priorities, and does not create an unnecessary barrier to progress.

As things stand, I remain comfortable with what we introduced in 1999, believing that it was the best possible solution to the competing demands of different constituencies. I must also acknowledge a degree of frustration at the delays in development and am impatient for change. Equally, I am excited by what I see when I look at what was once only the potential of ICT being realised and implemented by colleagues from awarding bodies and UfI/learndirect.

I am grateful for the opportunity NIACE has given me through this paper to attempt to set the record straight, to clarify misunderstandings and, where necessary, address misrepresentation. Whilst drafting the paper I have often found myself reflecting on the differences between policy and practice, between research and development and between theory and its implementation. In this context it is enlightening to reflect on a response given by the American pop artist, Claus Oldenburg, when asked by a friend if he was upset by a recent review of one of his exhibitions. He replied, 'Aesthetics to artists is like ornithology to birds'.[85]

It seems to me that much of this paper, and others like it, is about 'aesthetics' and 'ornithology'. Whatever our disagreements, whatever our personal ideologies, no one should doubt that learners are at the heart of the *Skills for Life* strategy; it is their voice and their experiences that matter. Given their positive response to the gremlins, their clear desire for qualifications and their acknowledged enthusiasm for ICT, we all, as policy makers owe it to them to take advantage of the unique opportunities created by *Skills for Life* to help them to seize the moment and progress: in Oldenburg's terms, enable them to fly.

Barry Brooks

---

85   Gauguin described the bird at the feet of the old woman in 'Where Do We Come From? …! as follows: 'a strange white bird … represents the futility of words'.

References

ALI (2003a) *Camden LEA Adult Community Learning Inspection Report* Adult Learning Inspectorate

ALI (2003b) *Islington LEA Adult Community Learning Inspection Report* Adult Learning Inspectorate

ALI/Ofsted (2003) *Literacy, numeracy and English for speakers of other languages: a survey of current practice in post-16 and adult provision* Adult Learning Inspectorate and Office for Standards in Education

Aniskowicz, B T (1994) Canadian Wildlife Service: *Hinterland Who's Who* Ministry of Supply and Services, Canada

ARG (1999) *Assessment for Learning: Beyond the Black Box* Assessment Reform Group, University of Cambridge School of Education

ARG (2002) *Testing, Motivation and Learning* Assessment Reform Group, University of Cambridge Faculty of Education

Beder H (1999) *The Outcomes and Impacts of Adult Literacy Education in the United States* National Centre for the Study of Adult Learning and Literacy

Black P & Wiliam D (1998) *Inside the Black Box: Raising Standards through Classroom Assessment* Kings College London

Boud D (2000) 'Sustainable development: rethinking assessment for the learning society' *Studies in Continuing Education* Vol 22/2

Coffield F (2000) *The Necessity of Informal Learning* Policy Press

Dewson S, Eccles J & Tackey N D (2000) *Measuring Soft Outcomes and Distance Travelled* Research Report 219 Department for Education and Employment

DfEE (1998) *The Learning Age: a Renaissance for a New Britain* Department for Education and Employment / HMSO

DfEE (1999) *Skills for Neighbourhood Renewal: Local Solutions, Final Report of the Policy Action Team on Skills* Department for Education and Employment

DfES (2001) *Skills for Life – the National Strategy for Improving Adult Literacy and Numeracy Skills* Department for Education and Skills DfES Publications

DfES (2002) *Success in Adult Literacy, Numeracy and ESOL Provision – A guide to support the Common Inspection Framework* Department for Education and Skills DfES Publications

DfES (2003a) The Skills for Life Survey: A National Needs and Impact Survey of Literacy, Numeracy and ICT Skills Department fo Education and Skills / HMSO

DfES (2003b) *Skills for Life – the National Strategy for Improving Adult Literacy and Numeracy Skills: Focus on Delivery to 2007* Department for Education and Skills DfES Publications

DfES / LSC (2003) Joint DfES/LSC Fact Sheet *Recording Adult Literacy, Language and Numeracy ('Basic Skills') Provision* (Learning and Skills Council, 20 March 2003) Bulletin 5

Ecclestone K (2002) *Learning Autonomy in Post-16 Education: The Politics and Practice of Formative Assessment* Routledge Falmer

Eraut M (2002) 'The interaction between qualifications and work-based learning' in K Evans, P Hodkinson and L Unwin (eds) *Working to Learn* Kogan Page

Evans K (2002) 'The challenge of "making learning visible": problems and issues in recognising tacit skills and key competences' in K Evans, P Hodkinson and L Unwin (eds) *Working to Learn* Kogan Page

FEFC (1998) *Basic Education*, Report from the Further Education Funding Council, April 1998

Fryer R H (1997) *Learning for the Twenty-first Century* NAGCELL (The National Advisory Group for Continuing Education and Lifelong Learning)

Greenwood M, Hayes A, Turner C and Vorhaus J (2001) *Recognising and Validating Outcomes of Non-accredited Learning: A Practical Approach* Learning and Skills Development Agency

Grief S and Windsor V (2002) *Recognising and Validating Learning Outcomes and Achievements in Non-accredited Basic Skills and ESOL* Learning and Skills Development Agency

Handy, Charles (1994) *The Empty Raincoat* Hutchinson, London

Kennedy H (1997) *Learning Works: Widening Participation in Further Education* Further Education Funding Council

LSDA (2002) 'Do summative assessment and testing have a positive or negative effect on post-16 learner' motivation for learning in the Learning and Skills sector?' At **http://www.lsrc.ac.uk/files/lsrc/tender3.doc**

Mace, J (2002) 'Can't someone in the real world write a proper test for literacy?' *The Guardian*, Tuesday May 28

McGivney V (2002) *A Question of Value: Achievement and Progression in Adult Learning* NIACE

Merrifield J (1998) *Contested Ground: Performance Accountability in Adult Basic Education* NCSALL Reports #1 (Cambridge MA)

Moser, Sir Claus (1999) *A Fresh Start: Improving Literacy and Numeracy.* Report of the Working Group, Department for Education and Skills

NIACE (2001) 'A Response to "Skills for Life", the national strategy for improving adult literacy and numeracy skills' At:
http://www.niace.org.uk/Organisation/advocacy/skillsforlife/Default.htm

Office of the Deputy Prime Minister (2002) *The Learning Curve*, Neighbourhood Renewal Unit

Ofsted (1998) *Review of Secondary Education in England, 1993–1997* Office for Standards in Education / Adult Learning Inspectorate

Perry A (2000) 'Performance indicators: *Measure for measure* or *A comedy of errors?*' in C Mager and P Robinson (eds) *The New Learning Market* ippr / FEDA

QCA (2000) *National standards for adult literacy and numeracy* Qualifications and Curriculum Authority

QCA (2003) *Assessment for Learning: Using Assessment to Raise Achievement in Mathematics at Key Stages 1, 2 and 3* Qualifications and Curriculum Authority

QCA website: National Adult Literacy and Numeracy Qualifications – Entry Level: At:
http://www.qca.org.uk/qualifications/types/595.html
http://www.qca.org.uk/qualifications/types/596_1351.html

Reder S (2002) 'Discussant notes from the ESRC Adult Basic Education seminar on Adult Basic Education as Social Practice' At **http://www.education.ed.ac.uk/hce/ABE-seminars/detail.html#1** October 2002

Sargant N, Field J, Francis H, Schuller T and Tuckett A (1997) *The Learning Divide* NIACE 1997

Sargant N (2000) *The Learning Divide Revisited* NIACE 2000

Sargant N & Aldridge F (2002) *Adult Learning and Social Division: A Persistent Pattern* NIACE

Sticht T G (1999) 'Testing and Accountability in Adult Literacy Education' At **www.nald.ca/fulltext/sticht/testing/cover.htm**

Taylor C (2002) *The Learning and Skills Council Adult Literacy and Numeracy Delivery Plan: A NIACE response* NIACE

Turner C (2001) Squaring the Circle: *Funding Non-accredited Adult Learning under the Learning and Skills Council* NIACE

Turner C and Tuckett A (2003) *Catching the Tide: A Paper Scoping Areas of Consensus and Debate in the Identification and Recording of Achievement in Non-certificated Learning* NIACE

Turner C and Watters K (2001) *Proof Positive: Learners' Views on Approaches to Identifying Achievement in Non-accredited Learning* NIACE

Uden A (2003) *Education and Training for Offenders* NIACE

Ward J and Edwards J (2002) *Learning Journeys – Learners' Voices: Learners' Views on Progress and Achievement in Adult Literacy and Numeracy* Learning and Skills Development Agency

Wiliam D (2001) 'What is wrong with our educational assessments and what can be done about it?', *Education Review* 15 (1), Autumn 2001

Other new NIACE policy discussion papers

Further Education and Adult Learning

Colin Flint, 2004, ISBN 1 86201 206 7

Adult Learners in a Brave New World – Lifelong learning policy and structural changes since 1997

Leisha Fullick, 2004, ISBN 1 86201 178 8

Learning's Not a Crime: Education and training for offenders and ex-offenders in the community

Tony Uden, 2004, ISBN 1 86201 207 5

niace

promoting adult learning